# Fulfilling Our Promise:
## Rotarians Volunteer in Kano, Nigeria

A journal by Norman Veliquette with
contributions by Kristin Duckart, Barbara Groner,
Sharon McKeown, Phillip Wise & Karien Ziegler

*"...Heartwarming, very enjoyable, 'must reading' for those interested in the fight to rid the world of polio."*

– Robert O. Brickman, PRIVP

Copyright 2003 by Norman Veliquette

All rights reserved. No part of this book may be reproduced or transmitted in any form or by any means, electronic or mechanical, including photocopying, recording, or by any information storage and retrieval system, without permission in writing from the publisher.

Published by The War on Polio Fund, Grand Traverse Regional Community Foundation, 250 E. Front St. Suite 310, Traverse City, MI 49684. Phone 231-935-4066 or fax 231-941-0021. War on Polio Fund passes all profits of this venture to The Rotary Foundation of Rotary International Polio Eradication Fund. Electronic order form available at the Grand Traverse Regional Community Foundation web site, http://www.gtrcf.org for orders in groups of ten copies. Inquiries to lsee@gtrcf.org.

Publisher's Cataloging-in-Publication Data:
Fulfilling Our Promise: Rotarians Volunteer in Kano, Nigeria
Veliquette, Norman     Traverse City, Mich., The War on Polio Fund, 2003
p.    cm.    ill.
1. Health - Polio/Nigeria
2. Nigeria/Health - Polio Eradication

ISBN #   0-9729836-0-0
LCCN # 2003661082

Project Coordination by Bookability, Inc.
P.O. Box 843 • Elk Rapids, Michigan 49629

Printed in the United States of America

*I am encouraged by my observations and experiences in Nigeria's Polio National Immunization Days, NIDs. Where climate, economy, politics, history, culture, and religion have created an environment of adversity, it is a unique experience to witness and be part of an idealistic global effort made realistic by courageous people of all skin colors and nationalities, all religious faiths, and all walks of life—men and women of all ages, rich and poor, joined in the War on Polio, committed to interrupting the transmission of the wild polio virus, eradicating the disease from the planet and sparing humanity from its life threatening and crippling effects forever. It is a story of leadership, courage, and strength in numbers.*

*The book that follows developed quickly and unexpectedly, representing the powerful and unexpected emotions we experienced during and following our return from Nigeria. We hope our account brings great, well-deserved satisfaction to all the supporters of the War on Polio. May it also build understanding and support for the leadership of 2003-04 Rotary International President Jonathan B. Majiyagbe from Kano, Nigeria.*

*The photo on the front cover, a casual shot taken at the National Flag-Off in Katsina, was selected weeks in advance of Jonathan Majiyagbe's unveiling of his RI presidential theme* Lend a Hand. *The similarities between the cover photo and Majiyagbe's logo were immediately striking, nurturing our growing conviction that "the Kano journal" is a Rotary story deserving to be told.*

*Thank you, Tom, Lou, and Martha for generous assistance in preparing the manuscript.*

*In addition to all that is obvious, this account benefits immensely from the input of my NID teammates and co-authors. I am profoundly grateful to Sharon, Karien, Kristin, Barb and Phil. In the fatigue and mesmerizing effects of a land where strange names, sights, sounds and circumstances swirl about, it is invaluable to have additional eyes, ears and memories at work together. However, I accept full responsibility for this work and ask forbearance and forgiveness for any unforeseen and unintended consequences resulting from errors of statement or omission. – NRV*

*Dedicated to Dave and Barbara Groner, both members of the Rotary Club of Dowagiac, Michigan. On three occasions prior to Nigeria, the Groners led missions of National Immunization Days volunteers to India. Before the ink is dry on this manuscript, they will lead another North American group of more than 60 volunteers to the populous State of Uttar Pradesh in central India. Personally and collectively, on behalf of the entire polio eradication campaign, we thank and honor them for their thoughtful, unselfish, and courageous leadership.*

# Rotary's Polio Initiative

Rotary International is comprised of over 30,100 local clubs with 1.2 million members in 163 countries. It is one of the largest non-profit service organizations in the world, founded in Chicago, Illinois, USA in 1905.

In 1985, Rotary International spearheaded Polio-Plus, a global initiative to immunize all of the world's children against polio. Its goal was and continues to be the worldwide eradication of polio by Rotary's centennial year, 2005.

To date, the program has immunized more than two billion children in 122 countries, reducing the incidence of polio by more than 99%. Through fundraising, technical support, and political collaboration, the program has provided polio vaccine, operational support, medical personnel, laboratory equipment and educational materials for health workers and parents.

With its community-based network worldwide, Rotary is the volunteer arm of a global partnership dedicated to eradicating polio. Local and international Rotary volunteers assist in vaccine delivery, social mobilization and logistical help, cooperating with national health ministries, the World Health Organization (WHO), UNICEF, and the U.S. Centers for Disease Control and Prevention.

Eradication of polio is one of the most ambitious humanitarian undertakings ever, leaving as a legacy a blueprint for public and private collaborations in humanitarian work worldwide.

*–Sharon McKeown*

# Foreword

When Rotary International (RI) launched PolioPlus in 1985, over 1000 children **a day** were being paralyzed by polio throughout the world.

I was a participant in the initial meeting between representatives of RI and the staff at the U.S. Centers for Disease Control and Prevention (CDC). I clearly recall the dedication and commitment of the representatives of RI as they persuaded CDC to join them in eliminating polio. A partnership was forged there that has been critical to the progress toward successfully eliminating polio. Rotary International was instrumental in expanding the partnership to include WHO and UNICEF as well.

Since 1985, there have been tens of thousands of Rotarians involved with Polio eradication, and they are responsible for having the goal of eradication within our grasp. In 2002, there were an estimated 1500 cases in only seven countries **for the whole year**. One of the countries was Nigeria, and nearly one-half of the cases in Nigeria occurred in the northern states of Kano and Kaduna.

Norm Veliquette and his team of six North American Rotarians take us along for their week as volunteers to the State of Kano and show us, up close and personal, the work of polio elimination. They clearly reveal the complex societal structure of northern Nigeria. And from their journal, we learn the importance of local and visiting Rotarians in influencing traditional leaders – from their audience with the Emir to issues of mismanagement at the ward level. The team shows us how the program works and why difficulties remain because of culture and past experiences with health care institutions.

Norm and his team share with us the places, people, humor and dangers that accompany this most serious work. This account, *Fulfilling Our Promise: Rotarians Volunteer in Kano, Nigeria*, demonstrates the dedication and humanitarian spirit of Rotarians across the world.

*Robert J. Kingon*

*Deputy Director, Policy, Planning, and Evaluation (retired)*
*Centers for Disease Control and Prevention*
*Atlanta, GA*

# ROTARY INTERNATIONAL

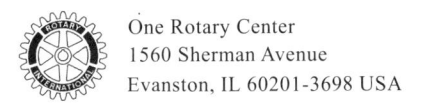

One Rotary Center
1560 Sherman Avenue
Evanston, IL 60201-3698 USA

**JONATHAN B. MAJIYAGBE**
President, 2003-04

The remark is often made that wherever there are challenges, Rotarians see these as opportunities for service. The ongoing campaign to rid the world of polio is a brilliant example of this important statement.

Whereas the story of polio is a melancholic catalogue of maiming and death for young children and despair and desolation for their parents, the eradication of the dreaded disease has provided opportunities for Rotarians to reach out across the miles and lend a hand during National Immunization Days to save defenseless children from the crippling disease. This was exactly the humanitarian service that a North American Rotary Volunteer team carried out in Kano, Nigeria some weeks back.

It was thankfully an example of Rotary in action, touching lives, affecting people, and I am sending this note in appreciation of the selfless service of the Rotary Volunteers from North America.

Sincerely,

Jonathan B. Majiyagbe
President-elect, Rotary International

## Contents

How It All Starts . . . . . . . . . . . . . . . . . . . . . . . . . . . . 13

November 5: Tuesday . . . . . . . . . . . . . . . . . . . . . . . 15

November 6: Wednesday . . . . . . . . . . . . . . . . . . . . 21

Polio . . . . . . . . . . . . . . . . . . . . . . . . . . . . . . . . . . . . . 28

November 7: Thursday . . . . . . . . . . . . . . . . . . . . . . 29

Meet the Kano Team . . . . . . . . . . . . . . . . . . . . . . . 33

November 8: Friday . . . . . . . . . . . . . . . . . . . . . . . . 38

November 9: Saturday . . . . . . . . . . . . . . . . . . . . . . 43

November 10: Sunday . . . . . . . . . . . . . . . . . . . . . . 51

Cold Chain . . . . . . . . . . . . . . . . . . . . . . . . . . . . . . . 59

November 11: Monday . . . . . . . . . . . . . . . . . . . . . 68

November 12: Tuesday . . . . . . . . . . . . . . . . . . . . . 73

November 13: Wednesday . . . . . . . . . . . . . . . . . . 90

November 14: Thursday . . . . . . . . . . . . . . . . . . . . 99

Getting the Job Done . . . . . . . . . . . . . . . . . . . . . 113

November 15: Friday . . . . . . . . . . . . . . . . . . . . . . 115

November 16: Saturday . . . . . . . . . . . . . . . . . . . 124

Y3K Chatter: Post Operation . . . . . . . . . . . . . . . 129

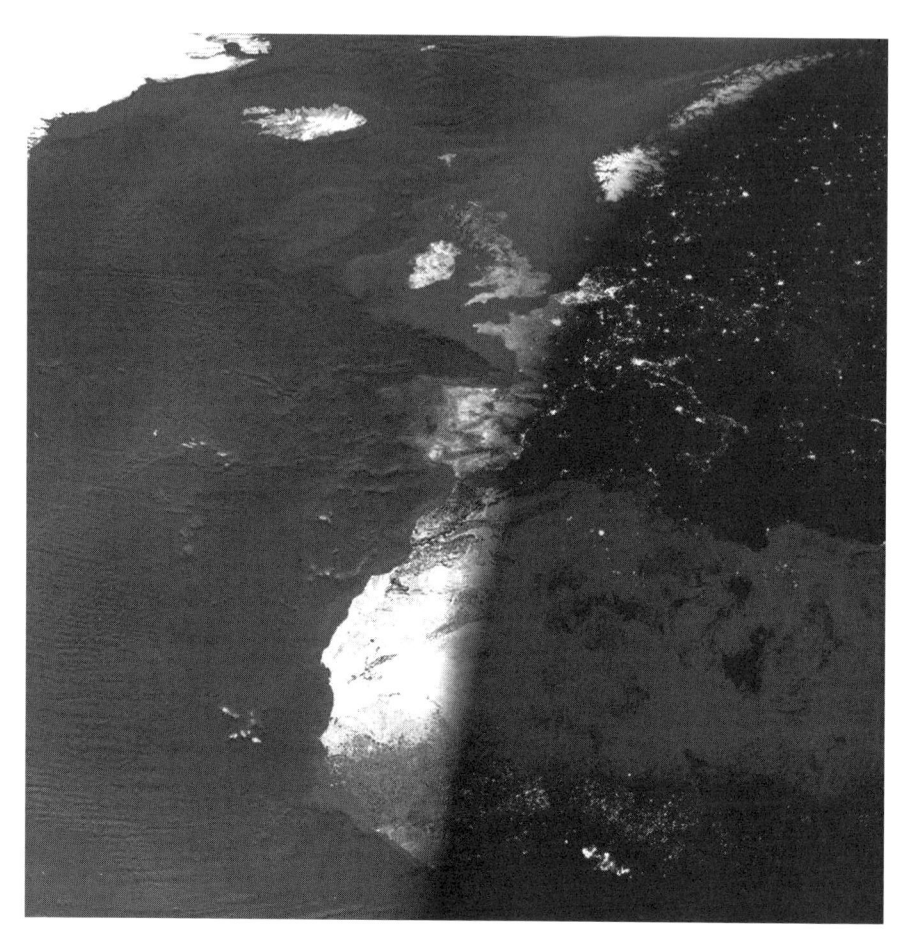

*"Sunset from Space" taken via satellite: A unique perspective on that part of the world over which the NID Volunteers flew on the way to and from their mission. The line of demarcation between sunlight and darkness is approximately the air route between Amsterdam and Lagos. Note the Sahara can be seen clearly both during daytime and nighttime. The magnitude of the Sahara stretching across Africa plays into the theme of the Kano journal. Perhaps there is moonlight, as on the night the volunteers flew home. The lights of Lagos and Port Harcourt in southern Nigeria are prominent. Abuja, Enugu and Kano are not as distinct. On top, to the left, is Greenland, totally frozen.*

# How It All Starts

Chatting by e-mail for several weeks, members of the team going to Kano, nearly 1,000 kilometers north of Lagos, become acquainted and share internet research before actually meeting. Kano denotes both Kano State and it's capital, the City of Kano, in northern Nigeria. We learn the day before departure that our itinerary will include a visit to the Emir of Kano. "What is an emir? Who is the Emir of Kano?"

In minutes, the internet provides answers. We instantly share the information, *and we know* that going to Kano will be special! We learn that there have been alarming new outbreaks of polio in Northern Nigeria. *Or,* is it that surveillance is getting better at detecting and confirming polio cases?

Strategically, we are four women and two men: Barb Groner, co-leader with Norm Veliquette; Kristin Duckart, Wisconsin Rapids, Wisconsin; Sharon McKeown, Windsor, Ontario, Canada; Dr. Karien Ziegler, West Orange, New Jersey; Dr. Phil Wise, Grand Rapids, Michigan.

We are part of a much larger group, 40 Rotary Volunteers, pulled together by past district governor (PDG) Dave Groner and his wife Barbara. Dave and Barb met PDG Ade Adefeso from Lagos, Nigeria, and his wife Bola at the 2002 Rotary International Convention in Barcelona, Spain. Together, they agreed on the parameters of this mission: forty North American Rotary Volunteers would visit Nigeria during the November 2002 National Immunization Days (NIDs) for polio. They would form seven teams: four would stay in Lagos and three would go to remote cities. Local Rotarians in each city would host them and determine their itineraries.

Dave and Barb gave much consideration to assignments, which volunteers to put on each team. The final selections for the team going to Kano in the north are very different from the originals. Four women were added, four men were deleted. Barb Groner will go with the Kano team and Dave will stay in Lagos.

Predominantly Islamic people inhabit northern Nigeria. A man may not enter another man's home without the homeowner's presence and a woman may not touch or look upon a man other than her husband. Strict laws of the Islamic Sharia have been adopted by about a dozen of Nigeria's northern states. Sharia is based on the Koran and the traditional sayings of the Prophet Mohammed, urging the formation of a theocratic state. We endorse Dave and Barb Groner's strategy of having a female majority on the Kano team. It should make the team more appealing and less threatening in the Islamic neighborhoods of Kano.

It's expected that the campaign to eradicate polio will involve going house-to-house to find and vaccinate the children, an estimated population of 3.8 million under 5 years of age in Kano State—10% of the national total. It is such a large number that we wonder if we might have misunderstood.

Nigeria has earned the reputation of an ugly place. A savage civil war in the late 1960's was followed by nearly 30 years of military governments. In the past three years, a spiral of ethnic disturbances and religious bloodletting has claimed an estimated 10,000 lives, including the life of Andrew Gana.

Andrew was the son of Francis and Winifred Gana, dear friends of my wife Marjory and me. Andrew was the same age as our son Roger. We have daughters the same age as the two daughters of Francis and Winnie. The Ganas live in Kaduna, a city in north central Nigeria, a two and one half hour drive south of Kano. Andrew was shot at the gate of his father and mother's house during the sectarian crisis that engulfed Kaduna in February 2000. He had graduated from the university a year earlier; finished the mandatory Youth Service Corps on February 18, 2000 was shot on the 21st and died on the 22nd.

My friendship with the Ganas influenced Dave and Barbara Groner to assign me to the Kano team. One of my objectives in Nigeria is to make a social connection with Francis and Winnie. They know that I am coming. Francis and I served the same year as Rotary district governors in our respective districts. We and our wives met in Anaheim, California during our training at Rotary's International Assembly in February 1993.

Friends at home asked me frequently before leaving if I feared for my safety. Often I was told, "Be careful." Native Rotarians, said to be in the top socio-economic strata, will accompany us. We will do the work they have arranged for us and surrender ourselves to their care.

# November 5: Tuesday

Our group of 40 assembles for the first time at the airport in Amsterdam, most arriving on overnight flights from various North American cities, including Canadian locations. Group leader Dave Groner tells us that no group of volunteers as large as ours has ever visited Nigeria to eradicate polio.

Barb Groner gives a yellow tee shirt to each volunteer. On the dark blue collars and on the blue trim of their sleeves the shirts have decorative trim. They have a matching blue Polio Plus logo of The Rotary Foundation on their fronts. We pull them on--and we look good!

Ready, we fly out together, heading south across France and over the Pyrenees Mountains. Carol Mitchell, my Rotary Club-mate from Elk Rapids proclaims their beauty from her window seat. Then come Spain, the Mediterranean Sea, and finally Africa!

It's mid-afternoon. The sun has been beating on the Sahara Desert yet another day, raising clear thermal columns even into the seven-mile high zone through which we are flying. The ride is rough.

Everyone notices weather. But on the farm back home weather is either a friend or a foe, and I study weather as a sentinel surveys the horizon. Meteorologists watch the atmospheric disturbances coming off the west coast of Africa as indicators of tropical storms in the Atlantic. The disturbances drift from the Sahara westward across the ocean, gathering energy and humidity from the warm waters of the western Atlantic, Caribbean Sea, and Gulf of Mexico, sometimes becoming hurricanes that strike North America. The world is all tied together; to understand how is our challenge and privilege.

The "desert view" compels many of the North Americans to get up from their seats and lean across to the windows where they peer down on an endless expanse of textured and sculpted sand. Northern Nigeria reaches to the southern fringes of this continental wasteland. What will the Kano team see there?

The afternoon sun casts a perfect light on the relief of the rolling and variegated landscape below. The magnitude of it escapes comprehension. We fly on, another four hours to Lagos.

I'm sitting next to a young black man who introduces himself as Benjamin from North Carolina: 39 years old, single, a physician, eyeglasses, head cleanly shaved, a polished look. He is returning to Enugu, Nigeria, to mourn and bury his father, killed in a traffic accident a month ago. The body has been in a morgue for a month. Benjamin was a small boy during the Biafra war of secession in the 1960's. His father was in Germany at the time and survived the war by staying there.

Benjamin remembers neighborhood friends as young as 12 being conscripted as soldiers to the Igbo cause. He remembers hiding in the basement with his mother and brothers when the conscriptors would come through. "By the time the war front reached Enugu, we (Biafrans) were done," he said. "We went back to the village of Shiala."

Benjamin went on to say the Biafran secession was doomed to failure from the start. It wasn't very well thought out. No one factored in the power of oil in the geopolitics of the situation. He observes, and probably correctly, that as long as there are resources in sub-Saharan Africa coveted by powerful entities from other places, those powers will promote "endemic warfare" among the competing Africans. Oil, diamonds, tin, manganese, and gold will be among the spoils.

Pizza is served for dinner as the sun sets on the desert. The western horizon exhibits a series of chimney-like clouds that wisp up from the land and off at the top as mare's tail cirrus clouds, their dark images against the pink backdrop of the sunset. The cloud images undoubtedly mark powerful updrafts off the desert floor. Nigerians call the hot, dry desert wind blowing from the desert, the *harmattan*.

Benjamin takes out his laptop and studies for a medical board exam. He explains a few case questions to me. We speculate what our grandfathers, his and mine, black and white, would think to see their grandsons visiting cordially over a small computer on a platform with 400 other humans seven miles above the African Continent. The words "science" and "magic" would be used.

**We are greeted in Lagos** by a score of Rotarians. Their faces are so *black,* accentuated by the bright yellow vests and yellow baseball hats used by Rotary volunteers in the NIDs—a beautiful sight—colorful, smiling and welcoming. As we wait for luggage, Dave Groner's counterpart, Ade Adefeso, hands me a cell phone and says, "Biodun Sanwo wants to talk to you." It's noisy in the terminal and except for "Welcome to Nigeria," I am unable to understand the excited voice that crackles on the phone.

Biodun Sanwo was one of Rotary International's district governors in 1993-94. Biodun served in Rotary District 9110 here in Lagos while I was Governor in District 6290 back home, and Francis Gana served in District 9120 in northern Nigeria. We were three of Rotary's 505 district governors that year. For this reason, we call ourselves classmates. We served under the same Rotary International president. We wore jackets of the same color and style, we proclaimed the same Rotary theme, at the same time, in different corners of the world.

*November 5*

Biodun and I sat literally next to each other as classmates in a small workshop session at the International Assembly in Anaheim, California in February 1993. I cannot remember the name of another person in that classroom. Francis Gana was not in our workshop. Why and how I remember Biodun seems a fateful coincidence. I wrote and told him I was coming to Nigeria for the National Immunization Days, NIDs, but heard nothing in return. What a pleasant courtesy that he should be waiting by his phone and call when I arrive!

Our luggage is an embarrassing spectacle, tons of large, heavy bags, explained in part, and perhaps mitigated by the fact that everyone has a heavy load of "slightly used" children's clothing to be presented to local Rotarians for charity.

The welcoming Rotarians have provided, or allowed, manpower and modern new buses to transport us to the hotel. It's dark, 8:30 to 9:00 p.m. It has rained and in places the streets are flooded. We look through the beaded water on the bus windows. On high spots, vendors in the flickering light of large candles are displaying breads, fruits and packaged goods. The darkness is filled with life, and perhaps—surely—death too. It is somber to imagine life outside the bus. Finding a clean and dry place to eat, sleep and dispose of life's waste products—impossible.

The luggage scene is repeated at the Airport Hotel where we unload, sort and lug our bags to our pre-assigned rooms. We don't have local currency. No one knows whether the porters have been hired by our hosts, whether or not to tip, how much, etc. From our numbers, a group develops at the hotel restaurant. Cold water, cold beer, and small talk settle us down before we retire to our first night in Africa.

Dr. Phil Wise from Grand Rapids is my roommate. He assembles the water filter he brought from his camping gear, pumping us each a bottle of safe drinking water. When I tell him that I worry about constipation as much as diarrhea while traveling, he says he will give me two tablespoons of unfiltered tap water if I have trouble with constipation. On the other hand, he thinks the coarse local toilet paper ought to discourage me from having the problem of diarrhea. I'm glad my travel mate is a doctor. He came prepared: four rolls of the soft stuff from home.

Phil, 48, is a can-do person, a surgeon, actually a urologist—a plumber of human anatomy. He grew up on the West Coast, a surf-city kid, likes camping and skiing, graduated from the University of Southern California, School of Medicine in 1982—and his father before him, in 1946. Phil's been on medical missions to Mexico; with him, poverty and disease have no shock value. He's incredibly direct, but a great humorist as well; he frequently floats an outrageous trial balloon, and I quickly catch on that he's not always serious. But sometimes he is, and that worries me a little. We're going to Kano, the Islamic north; as both his roommate and the team leader, I will be responsible for this Christian jokester.

We share that neither of our wives took much initiative to send us here; both acquiesced to the principle that what we've come to do is noble work. They both support our conviction to plunge in and do something. My wife Marjory has a kidney transplant and her immune system is medically suppressed to prevent rejection of the foreign organ. Otherwise, she'd be here. We met as youth exchange students in the mid 1960s. I went to Brazil, she to Nepal.

Phil is still in love with Sue, the woman he met while in residency in Houston in 1983. He married her and they have three children. He pulls out a poem Sue gave him, and shows it to me. It's the poem that tipped the balance in favor of his coming to

Nigeria:

> *If they would find a cure when I'm a kid...*
> *I could ride a bike and sail on roller blades, and*
> *I could go on really long nature hikes.*
> *If they would find a cure when I'm a teenager...*
> *I could earn my license and drive a car, and*
> *I could dance every dance at my senior prom.*
> *If they would find a cure when I'm a young adult...*
> *I could travel around the world and teach peace, and*
> *I could marry and have children of my own.*
> *If they would find a cure when I'm grown old...*
> *I could visit exotic places and appreciate culture, and*
> *I could proudly share pictures of my grandchildren.*
> *If they would find a cure when I'm alive...*
> *I could live each day without pain and machines, and*
> *I could celebrate the biggest thank you of life ever.*
> *If they would find a cure when I'm buried into Heaven,*
> *I could still celebrate with my brothers and sisters there,*
> *And I could still be happy knowing that I was part of the effort.*
> *— Author unidentified*

Grateful for the unlimited supply of safe water that the pump will provide, I fish in my bag and give Phil some of the dried cherries left over from those I handed out to the NID Group in Amsterdam. I have a few more that I can ration as personal gifts to my teammates and special hosts through the week.

The room has air-conditioning and we sleep well.

## November 6: Wednesday

We awake at dawn. Our window is facing the morning sky, east. Spreading the curtains of our second floor room, I can see human silhouettes moving about in the narrow alley outside the wall of the hotel compound. In the gray morning light the figures take shape and give meaningful gestures – stretching, greeting, etc. A heavy woman in a light colored smock comes and stands on one leg at the corner, resting the other on a bench. She appears to be organizing people's day. As others pass, their lives seem to take on purpose, speeding up their gait, getting buckets, tubs, pans, canisters, heading off as if to fetch water. Lagos is built on the flat coastal plain of West Africa. 100-foot towers dot the cityscape as far as the horizon. Below the towers, one and two-story buildings are packed together, covered by corrugated metal roofs. They have a rusty look, but many sport antennas. "For what?" I wonder, "TVs, computer satellite uplinks?" I marvel at the dispersion of communications technology. As the sun rises, its rays are scattered by the grime on our window and it becomes difficult to view the city against the light.

Phil and I each get 13,500 Nigerian naira for US$100. The Bureau de Change is a small room, little bigger than a phone booth, among some shops within the hotel compound. A personable Rotarian, Bankole "Banky" A.D. Shonubi, accompanies us, implying that we'll get a fair shake in his presence, suggesting some risk without a local witness.

We pay cash for our meals and personal purchases, but for our rooms and in-country travel, our money was forwarded to Ade Adefeso's National Polio Committee. By utilizing the National Polio Plus Committee, he saved us nearly half on the cost of our hotel rooms. It's not clear whether the hotels made the concession or whether the National Polio Committee has supplemented our funds. Breakfast in the hotel restaurant cost 10,000 naira, about $7.50.

Mike is another of the most outgoing of the welcoming Rotarians. He and Banky take us on a group walk through the nearby market. They warn us sternly about taking pictures in potentially unfriendly environments. I hope my roommate Phil is listening, with his backpack full of photographic equipment, loaded like a Sherpa. If his equipment isn't stolen first, he's sure to get us in trouble. He can't carry all that equipment around and just not use it!

It's on my conscience now that I called him at home when he was packing. I threw out a challenge to him for some special photography: The November 2002 *Rotarian* magazine had just come out, publishing a full page photo of my 2000 hand-walk at the reflecting pool in front of the Taj Mahal. I made note to Phil that the photo had been taken by my son Roger, and Roger would not be along in Nigeria. "I certainly don't take any pictures of myself hand-walking; can I count on you...?" The answer was "yes." Now as I look at Dr. Wise's backpack full of cameras, I wonder if I have actually brought this on the two of us. He probably has visions of doing a *cover* photo for *The Rotarian*. And, how can I be sorry if he succeeds?

The walk of two blocks along and across busy thoroughfares is hazardous from the traffic, lack of sidewalks, and open sewers. But, the market is welcoming and friendly. Retailers of shoes, fabrics, beauty and personal care products, beverages, and other miscellaneous goods are organized into sections. As retailers do, they smile and pose for photos with us and with their wares.

An outdoor spiritual assembly develops under two large tents in the center of the market. The music is contagious, wafting out into the nearby neighborhoods—a great attraction to the market. It touches people in the market too, as those in the shops sing, clap, and dance to the rhythms coming from the tents. People are all smiles, returning eye contact and greetings. As the presence of our large group permeates the market, people begin to ask us to take their pictures. We are getting more attention than is comfortable, and we suspect it is time to leave.

**Beggars crippled by polio** hang around the busy intersection by the market. One in particular catches our attention. His flaccid legs are crossed and he seems attached to a small platform resembling a skateboard. He propels himself along the busy street with his hands, protected by rubber sandals, the shower thongs we used to call Zorries. Tom Dalton, an NID groupmate from Fort Myers, Florida, who will be staying in Lagos,

***Norm with Monsuru**: Norm makes an acquaintance with Monsuru, a polio victim who survives his crippled legs by begging in the streets of Lagos.*

makes an acquaintance with this street crawler, learning that his name is Monsuru, 18 years old. Tom will see him later in the week, and will show him, with poignant irony, the vaccine bottles and droppers from which children now receive protection against such crossed legs.

Yellow vans, their sides bumped and bruised in traffic, serve as taxis and buses. With narrow wooden benches for seats, they carry an astonishing number of passengers. In the high heat index of Lagos, their sliding side doors are either gone or left open as passengers pack themselves in to reach their destinations.
Back at the Airport Hotel, I peek out at the alley that I watched come to life this morning. It's vacant now except for the large trunk of a palm tree—no top, just a tall stump, maybe done in when the alley around it was paved. Biodun Sanwo calls again, this time with an invitation to dinner at his home; and would I also bring a couple of my teammates? I invite Phil and Kristin.

4:00 to 6:00 p.m.: Local Rotarians and their young associates, the Rotaractors, hold a reception for us by the swimming pool. The current governor of the local Rotary District welcomes us, lots of pictures are taken, a few speeches, niceties, etc. There are three other Rotary Districts in Nigeria. One or more of our teams will go to each district. Dave Groner gives his counterpart Ade Adefeso a yellow tee shirt like the ones that he and Barb have provided to the North American Volunteers. Dave and Ade have brought us together; they are everyone's heroes, stars of the show.

At 7:00 p.m., Biodun Sanwo's driver picks up Kristin, Phil and me. Security guards at the hotel gate stop us from leaving. They have orders not to let any of the white people out without authorization and proper accompaniment. Our Rotarian hosts have given this order with our safety in mind. I see Banky Shonubi nearby and he intervenes so that we may leave. We drive south a half-hour, being stopped more than once by officers in the highway, guns at-the-ready. The driver is vague when asked about the purpose of the checkpoint. Finally we arrive at the Sanwo home, not far from the port.

They receive and welcome us. Power is off. The Sanwos are apologetic. NEPA officially stands for Nigeria Electric Power Authority. They humor us that it really means Never Expect Power Anytime. For a couple of hours, we sit conversing in the dim candlelight of their elegant living room. The faces of our hosts are black. Only when we are close together can our eyes make out the details of their faces. In acts of mutual faith, animated and friendly conversation proceeds between silhouettes. To Biodun's and my left, Ayo and the girls befriend Kristin. Phil and the general surgeon share stories to our right, almost as unseen and uncounted friends in remote corners of the planet.

It is a powerful reunion evening—me with my 1993-94 district governor classmate Biodun and his wife Ayo—shared by a grandchild, fellow Rotarians and my teammates. Biodun and Ayo have seven children; "We're Catholic," he explains. I tell him, "I'm the oldest of 12; my parents were Catholic too." All of his seven children have received a good education and are now living outside the country.

As the evening wears on and our affection builds, Biodun begins to refer more frequently to himself as Joseph, his Christian name. Not one to cultivate talk of religion, I let the coincidence pass without remark that my baptismal patron is also Joseph.

Perhaps only the pictures will hint at the quality of the fellowship. Ayo's delicious cooking, plentiful beverages, and the unbeatable friendship of Rotary home hosting—a complete thought. And then the centerpiece of the evening: Ayo serves dinner on plates decorated with cherries and a cherry pie recipe. That my life's work has been shaped around cherries and that she should have cherry pie plates in the house is only one of several coincidences that have gone off the charts about our reunion. It must have been destiny that I should meet Joseph Biodun Sanwo again.

The Sanwos import fish from the North Sea. Not surprisingly, dinner consists of smoked mackerel, potatoes, spicy vegetables, plantains, chicken, hot sauce – Ayo's cooking.

I ask about their lives during the Biafra war of secession. Their stories are a mix of humor and tragedy. They were young then, impressionable. The Biafran ambassador stayed at the Sanwo home and is remembered best for having said, "When the time comes that I cannot have wine with my dinner, this war will have to stop!"

Power eventually comes on. We exchange gifts, Ayo giving me two of her cherry plates as gifts for my wife Marjory back in Elk Rapids, Michigan. I hand-walk, giving Biodun a preview of the picture he will see of his old classmate in the November edition of the *Rotarian* magazine when it reaches Nigeria, he thinks, in early December.

At about 11:30 p.m. they drive us back to the hotel. Joseph Biodun accompanies us, along with the general surgeon Rotarian and the driver. Later we speculate as to whether their accompaniment was a normal courtesy or a security measure on our behalf. We pass huge wholesale markets where hundreds of large trucks from the port are waiting in the darkness to discharge their cargoes. Retailers and distributors from the city will buy them tomorrow.

# POLIO
### By Phil Wise, MD

*P*oliomyelitis is a disease caused by the wild poliovirus, WPV. It is transmitted via the fecal-oral route. Poor sanitation in the form of open sewers and little water contributes to the spread of the disease. Children play in the street next to the sewers, getting fecal microbes from the street on their hands, and not being too particular about washing their hands before eating, the children ingest some of the microbes when they eat. The virus goes to the intestine, and multiplies. The infected child may develop a case of chronic diarrhea, sending the virus back to the gutter to infect someone else. The virus doesn't last too long in the wild; it needs a human host to survive. Thus, when the transmission of the virus is sufficiently interrupted by widespread immunizations, it dies and disappears from the environment.

Sometimes the virus goes through the intestinal wall of the host and attacks the spinal cord or central nervous system, causing damage to the nerve cells, which then die. The nerve death means that the muscles the nerve stimulated can no longer contract; they are paralyzed. The part paralyzed is determined by the nerve attacked. Sometimes it's one leg or the other or both; sometimes it's the arm; occasionally it would be the muscles that cause air to go in and out of the lungs, but it can strike any nerve that causes a muscle to contract.

The paralyzed victim is said to have acute flaccid paralysis, AFP. There are other causes of acute flaccid paralysis that are not caused by the poliomyelitis virus, Gillain-Barre and transverse myelitis are two that immediately come to mind. So an accurate diagnosis and response to the problem requires an on-going survey of the population for AFP, then sampling the stools of suspected cases to see if the polio virus is the actual cause. This requires a collection and delivery system for the fecal samples along with rather sophisticated laboratory instrumentation.

Since the virus can also occur in different subtypes, the fight against polio includes not only the mass vaccination of the population, but the accurate and immediate reporting of cases of AFP, as well as microbiological and virological study of the feces of subject cases: surveillance. One aspect of our mission will be looking for evidence of this surveillance system in Nigeria. Some speculate that the recent increase in the reported number of confirmed polio cases more accurately reflects an improvement in surveillance rather than an absolute increase in polio. It is not possible to conclude with certainty that the cases of polio have actually increased in the last year, but the surveillance system is finding more cases and reporting them. The recognition and definition of a problem is an essential prelude to remedying it.

Immunization is accomplished by giving children a live, but weakened, strain of the poliovirus, i.e. oral polio vaccine, OPV, which does not attack the nerve system, but which elicits an immune response against even WPV.

## November 7: Thursday

Among the 40 Rotarians in our group, many are Type A personalities, eager to start work. But, the National Immunizations Days do not begin until Saturday. Today will be another day for touring, for orientation, and for publicity.

Two comfortable tour buses take us to the National Museum. Several Nigerian Rotarians and Rotaractors accompany us. The powerful voice of Rotaractor Deyemi Bajo Ogunkoya leads us in singing familiar Rotary and camp songs as our buses meter their way to the downtown area of Lagos.

As the group gathers and waits for admittance to the museum, school children are also gathered, waiting for tour guides. I hand-walk; Dave Groner narrates. In the curiosity and reactions of the children, my travelmates and the Nigerians see the connection between hand-walking and polio.

The exhibits are simple and few, but rich in the heritage of the land. We see artifacts of daily life from the villages –foods, tools, masks, symbols of authority – things I read about only days ago in the book *Things Fall Apart* by famous Nigerian author Chinua Achebe. My Kano teammate, Karien Ziegler remarks, "So little of their past is intact, save their knowledge of it."

A British woman, a retired curator who has lived and traveled in Nigeria, has just opened a showroom where local artists display and sell their work. Knowing the artists and their lack of opportunity to show-and-tell, or sell, their works, she tells us she has planned this exhibit for several years and just opened it a day or so before our arrival. Our group is among the first to have access to this unique display. The NID group dutifully lines up and makes many purchases.

While part of the group shops for artwork, others mingle with school groups who have come to see the museum. Under the watchful eye of their teachers, students in one of the groups start tentatively touching me, maybe the first white man they have ever seen. Eye contact and an exchange of smiles with the teacher tells me this is a teaching moment, an unexpected aspect of the field trip for her students. The students are healthy and in the clean uniforms of their school. They are disciplined; touching them is a pleasant experience, but one that disarms me for another to come next week, among some older and not-so-mild-mannered children in the streets of Kano.

Showing off a good find from the museum shop as she gets on the bus, Karien assesses the choices she had: "The quality of the works range in my humble opinion from adequate to outstanding," leaving it for us to compliment her on recognizing which to buy.

We return to the hotel and give a press conference about National Immunization Days, NIDs. Ade Adefeso, chair of the National Polio Plus Committee, speaks, along with Dave Groner and others. As the questions and responses run their course, I dress and stretch in the back of the room, preparing for a high profile hand-walk. The Nigerians sense an opportunity and signal Dave Groner to bring me on.

As Dave narrates, considerably exaggerating my hand-walking exploits, I manambulate, a verb meaning to walk on one's hands, down the side aisle, cross in front, step over a coil of extension cords, camera cables, and finally stop after turning into the aisle on the other side. The cameras are all running and the audience erupts in enthusiastic applause. They offer me a microphone, "Perhaps you would like to make some comment?" I'm winded, but they are patient as I dedicate the effort to the children who might lose the use of their legs if we fail to deliver two drops of vaccine in their mouths. It's a showstopper. The main press conference adjourns as cameras and journalists surround me for further comments about using hand-walking for fundraising and raising awareness for polio eradication.

I started hand-walking at age 50, the result of a foolish challenge related to raising money for The Rotary Foundation while I was a Rotary district governor. Learning to walk on my hands was on my to-do list as a teenager and young man. Finally doing it gave me personal fitness along with a great deal of satisfaction. I kept it up; a couple hundred feet per day adds up to a mile a month, even allowing for a few days of rest. I estimate upwards of 70 miles over the past ten years. The biggest fundraising walk? $71,400 at the Rotary Zone 27-28 meeting in 2001. Scott Thigpen interviews me for U.S. public television. He represents CARE. His free-lance cameraman Gerard Dolan from Ottawa, Canada, operates Red Mango Pictures. Thigpen hired Dolan for this project. Greg Pope does Thigpen's sound and editing. Joy DeBenedetto, a young journalist from CNN is spending her vacation going to northern Nigeria as one of the CARE film team. Rotary International in Evanston has also put Jean-Marc Giboux, a free-lance photojournalist on assignment in Kano. One feels at every turn that something big is about to break in Nigeria's North.

All the film people, photographers, and journalists will be shadowing us in Kano, producing the last documentary film for a series they have done on the effort to eradicate polio. *The Last Child: The Global Race to End Polio* has a target release date of April 2003. Thigpen's crew has interviewed other members of our team, focusing first on Kristin Duckart at her home in Wisconsin Rapids, Wisconsin, a young single mom with teenage boys. Kristin made Scott Thigpen spell his last name when he first called her. She wanted to be sure she had not misunderstood. We'll have their cameras in our faces from time to time, stitching the story together of Y3K (the team nickname among ourselves) coming together and executing its mission.

Barb Groner has color-coded the nametags of the seven teams. The Red, White, Blue, and Green Teams will stay in Lagos. The three traveling teams have yellow nametags. One Yellow Team is headed to Abuja, a new city, less than 15 years old, the capital of Nigeria, built near the geographic center of the country. It is modern and more prosperous than many other areas. Another Yellow Team is headed to Enugu, the capital city of the "former eastern region" that attempted in the 1960s to secede from Nigeria as the Nation of Biafra, an event that interfered with my graduate studies in economic development and profoundly altered the course of my life.

The third Yellow Team, that's us, Y3K, is destined for Kano, a city more than 500 miles north of Lagos, a region that is 90% Muslim, contrasted with the predominately Christian south.

Y3K meets for its first private team dinner. Barb hands out yellow polio vests and bright yellow hats, like the ones we have admired on the Nigerians. Now we will look like them. We review info that we have collected and shared via email about "the North." Y3K originated early in our emails as YK3. We would be going to K̲ano, and the 3rd team with Y̲ellow nametags. In our e-mail chatter, it was my attempt at a cute play on the Y2K millennium virus.

In the world of WPV and AFP, we would be an anti-virus. But team members remained mysteriously silent, I thought, maybe not catching on. Finally I realized they were politely ignoring the mistake of my getting the letters and numerals out of order. It'll be Y3K from here on. But no matter, YK3 or Y3K, today we are suddenly a team, bursting with the pride and honor at the privilege of being assigned to "the North."

During the afternoon press conference, Dr. Nehemie Mbakuliyemo, a World Health Organization official from Ruwanda explained that polio in Nigeria is largely a problem concentrated in a few areas of "the North." *The North* has achieved a mystique: the home of the incoming Rotary International president Jonathan Majiyagbe, a land of emirs, Islamic people, the dry *harmattan* blowing off the Sahara desert, a place far away, one of the world's last remaining hot spots for the transmission of WPV, wild polio virus. And, **we** have been chosen to go there!

## Meet the Kano Team
*by Phil Wise, MD*

**BARB:** Wife of the NID mission leader Dave Groner, Barbara has spent most of her adult life as a schoolteacher, librarian, or principal. Of medium height and with short brown hair, she describes herself as having the shoulders of a halfback. She squints through glasses, sometimes with a look honed by years of silencing rowdy fourth graders. After a while, to fill the time, we all open up to each other, and Barb never hesitates with her marvellous stories.

Barb has handpicked all the teams, and the one for Kano with special care. Since she has been on several NIDs before, the rest of us naturally look up to her for advice and guidance. Her pre-trip instructions were thorough, and not without a bit of levity. She and Dave make a natural team, he with the lofty ideas, she with the practical solutions. Her unflagging support and advance information smoothed the way for all the Rotary Volunteers.

Barb is a conversationalist. On one occasion, she interviews a local while the rest of the team head out for the first round of vaccinations. While Sharon, Jean-Marc and I stick like glue to the local houseguide and vaccinator, Barb is so involved that she doesn't see us leave. Norm, Kris, and Karien wait for Barb. The group I follow is soon around the corner looking for subjects to vaccinate. Forty-five minutes later, after a successful sojourn, we return curious to find out what the others have experienced. They have stayed put, waiting for Barb. I'm sure her roommate is treated to lots of late night conversation. Barb loves to shop and wins the coveted team award for most souvenirs.

**KRIS:** Kristin Duckart is Barb's roommate after we get to Kano. I first saw Kris in the Detroit airport, tall and well-conditioned. She said she has a personal trainer. With stylish short blond hair and mild, courteous manner, Kris is an immediate hit with all the members of the team. She's somehow connected with cranberries, a prominent and successful product in Wisconsin Rapids, Wisconsin.

Kris recently came into possession of a digital camera and made herself a student of the instruction manual. She will take some phenomenal photos during the campaign. Showing the camera's display screen, she will delight many of her subjects by instantly showing them their likenesses in the images she has captured. Using this technique on one occasion, she convinces a reluctant mother to allow her child to be vaccinated.

Kris is a single mom with two pre-teen boys. To make contact with them from time to time, she has rented a satellite phone. She generously makes the phone available to other members of the team. Unfortunately the first several calls are unsuccessful due to technical difficulties, something about the antenna requiring adequate contact with the phone body.

By the "luck" of the draw, Kris has no roommate in Lagos. To allay concerns about her being seen going to her room alone, each night one of the men on the team accompanies her to her room and makes sure that she is safely locked in. She laughs a little when I check under the bed that has a 3" clearance, and in the closet. I give Kris the award for most luggage. Her large red bags are easily recognized by the sag on the baggage carousel. The handles are broken after the first leg of the trip.

**KARIEN, a.k.a. KA, Dr. Z, or just D.R.Z.:** Karien from New Jersey is a vegetarian. Diarrhea is a team concern in Kano and Karien is the first to ask what **do** you call a vegetarian with diarrhea? A salad shooter. At first I am put off by her East Coast accent, a typical reaction by someone who grew up in southern California. East meets

West. Shortly though, we manage to overcome the language barrier and she wins me over; we become teammates, dancing a tango on her birthday.

Karien holds a doctorate in psychology and has an interesting set of spectacle holders to go with it. They are not the usual piece of nylon connected to the glasses passed around the back of the neck. No, they are attached just behind the hinges and dangle down to just above the collarbones. Only from there, yes, they drape over the shoulders and around the neck. In the part that hangs vertically are intercalated artistically bent wires that look like fine earrings. Indeed, people have commented on her "earrings" before realizing that they are actually tethers to keep track of her glasses.

Once Karien realizes that we are dyed-in-the-wool carnivores, she doesn't spend much time trying to make us vegetarians. And no, neither do I try to slip any beef bullion into her rice. Karien turns the big six-oh on the trip. Of average height and build, her posture reminds me of someone who has spent long hours taking notes as people confide in her. I think that she will give Kris advice on what to leave out of her suitcase on the next trip.

**SHARON:** It is difficult to write a snapshot of Sharon: so normal, about 5' 4", normal build, blonde hair, friendly, charming. She is everyone's idea of the girl next door. She has a quick smile and confesses that a few years ago she had some kind of neurological event from which she has totally recovered. Well almost. It takes me the longest time to realize, but when she gives a heart-felt laugh, her right eye opens just a little as her left eye squints in mirth, probably the only residual of her event. She has overcome all others.

Sharon won't let you forget two things: 1) she is a mother and 2) she is Canadian. During the Nigerian mission, we attend the meeting of a different Rotary Club almost daily. Without fail, we sing the Nigerian and United States national anthems, followed by "O Canada." By the end of the week, with Sharon's help, I actually know most of the words.

Before joining Rotary, Sharon traveled in Siberia as a member of a Rotary Group Study Exchange team, GSE. Ultimately, she joined the Rotary Club of Windsor, Ontario, and continues to be involved in GSE and Rotary Youth Exchange. Like Barb, she too is a shopper. Once, while going house-to-house vaccinating in a village, she stops to buy some fabric from a street vendor. It is just past noon; the local house guide and the vaccinator are calling it a day, the ice melting in their vaccine boxes. Sharon quickly strikes a deal with the merchant, buying the cloth without negotiating. She is doing her part to bring prosperity to this poor village.

Sharon is a Chartered Accountant, the Canadian equivalent of a CPA. She transcribes the rough draft of Norm's journal, setting a series of events in motion that unexpectedly leads to the evolution of this book. While she wins Miss Congeniality, the rest of us are runners-up.

**NORM:** The most difficult to characterize. My first encounter was a message he left on my answering machine at home. Actually we traded messages twice before having a conversation. He had been trying unsuccessfully to get me to respond to his broadcast emails. Barb had assigned us to room together, and not hearing from me, he had begun to wonder if I was a real person. Too bad, and unknown to him, he was addressing the communications to a recently disconnected mailbox. When he corrected the error, I was lucky enough to receive an instant replay from his outbox.

Norm asked about our motivation for going to Nigeria. I'm not hiding anything; I want to eradicate polio, perhaps deliver vaccine by camel to some of the nomadic Fulani tribes in the Sahara and maybe get an idea of what T.E. Lawrence wrote about in the Seven Pillars of Wisdom. Norm had planned to come to Nigeria as a graduate student of the agricultural sector in 1967, an adventure cancelled by the civil war that followed the Biafran succession. This journey might fulfill Norm's nagging curiosity about Nigeria, especially the North.

A Rotary leader, past district governor, obsessive journal writer, and one that requires only a little sleep, Norm assists the polio fundraising campaign by walking on his hands. The internationally distributed *Rotarian* magazine published a picture of him hand-walking in front of the Taj

Mahal. He senses opportunities to walk on his hands to create awareness for polio. After a walk of usually 50 to 70 steps, Norm dedicates that particular walk to all the children who might lose the use of their legs if we fail to deliver the polio vaccine.

Tallish, with a full head of prematurely white hair, Norm makes himself indispensable by offering to intervene at any time, any place to eradicate polio. Years of African interest have gone into this endeavor. He can tell you the elevation of the airport in Kano and uses words like "harmattan" and "emir" as if he grew up with them.

I sense at first that Norm feels a little insecure as the group leader, a cherry farmer leading 1) a woman with a Ph.D. in psychology, university professor; 2) a Canadian equivalent of a CPA, university professor; 3) the wife of the overall group leader, much more NID experience; 4) me, an MD, urologist, university professor; and 5) a woman whose association with Ocean Spray, synonymous with cranberry marketing success, makes cherry grower Norm green with envy.

Although he calls himself a cherry farmer, another member of the NID group says that Norm developed the processing side for probably the largest cherry operation in the U.S. He has our confidence. His suggestions and questions lead us to some rich discoveries of both the NID process and of ourselves.

Me? I'm **PHIL**, 5' 9" and a half inches tall, somewhere around 175 lbs. My hair used to be dark brown and thick. Now, it looks better if kept short. I like to swim, hike, snow ski and take photographs. My mother cared for polio victims in iron lungs as a nurse in Los Angeles during the decade of the 1940's. When Dave Groner gave a presentation at our Rotary Club in Grand Rapids requesting volunteers for a trip to eradicate polio, I was immediately interested. I like gadgets and only recently began to need glasses. I like to travel prepared, so I found a pair of reading glasses that fold into a small one and one-half inch blue aluminum container. Norm is relieved to find out it isn't a cigarette lighter. *Phil*

## November 8: Friday

We wait in the hotel lobby, bags packed, with sharp anticipation of our mission to Kano. Best wishes for a successful week are passing emotionally from team to team. Ade Adefeso casually hands me a brown bag and instructs me to give it to PDG Kola Owoka. "It's cash to pay for your hotel rooms and return tickets." I understand; Owoka will be our host in Kano. Cash is the only money in Nigeria, no credit cards, no checks. The circulation of so much untraceable value must contribute in a major way to bribery, corruption and theft, which is said to be common.

I confide to the team that my carry-on bag represents our return tickets. They understand and begin a watch that assures I give the bag safe passage to Kano. Banky and Mike taxi each of the traveling teams to the airport, taking the Enugu and Abuja teams, then returning for us.

As our flight on IRS Airlines heads north, the sprawling city of Lagos recedes from view, replaced by a beautiful, green, partially wooded, agricultural landscape, intermittently visible below through the scattered and steamy clouds. Look—red soil and palm trees. Breathe deeply, "This is Africa!"

We are seated together in the front row, three on each side of the aisle, heading north. Sharon, Karien, Kristin, Barb, Phil and Norm. "This is it, Team! From here on, we have a mission of our own!" If Barb had picked us on the basis of the poetry in our names, we could have been pleased. But, she had her reasons, and as we look at each other, we see Barb's vision, and we like what we see.

Scott Thigpen and his camera crew are on our flight, mixed somewhere among the passengers in the back. We land briefly in Abuja, the federal capital. The countryside here is characterized by large granite hills protruding from the guinea savannah. There are fewer and shorter trees than in the south, but intensive agriculture in small plots. Small villages characterize the habitation. Before we reach Kano, the countryside becomes dry and parched. Rains ended in September, six weeks ago. Trees are scattered. A hot wind, the *harmattan*, blows across the airport.

We let Scott's film crew deplane ahead of us. They plan to video us as we get off, but airport security guards object, the tip of an iceberg that the film crew will bump into in the days ahead.

As I deplane, Rabiu Isiyaku Rabiu, chairman of IRS Airlines, picks me out and introduces himself, asking about our flight. He's bursting with pride about his airplane. We are disappointed that Gerard couldn't take our pictures with his big camera. I tell Mr. Rabiu there might be a good thing he can do for a U.S. television crew, handing him over to Scott Thigpen. Rabiu is sympathetic and would like to have his airline featured in a US television documentary, but explains that no-pictures-at-airports is a carryover from military rule, a so-called national security issue.

We board a bus for a short ride to the terminal where a large welcoming party, singing Rotaractors and more reserved, but genuinely friendly Rotarian counterparts meet us. As if well rehearsed, they all address me as Pidiji Norm, accenting the first syllable of the titular acronym PDG for past district governor. We see new faces, hear new names, and begin molding new friendships. PDG Dr. Kolawole (Kola) Owoka is our lead contact. I inform him that I have money from Adefeso in Lagos.

They take us to the Prince Hotel, small, clean and modern in an out-of-the-way place, but in a gated compound nonetheless. It has a magnificent wooden staircase, corridors with marble floors, restaurant and pool. Although in a quiet neighborhood, a high wall, sharded with metal spikes and broken glass along the top, surrounds the compound. The gate, always attended, is closed except when vehicles enter or leave.

A man is posted at all times in each corridor outside the rooms; he is a sentry and a housekeeping person. We meet the young Lebanese man Tommy Solomon who owns and operates the hotel. He's a charming host, pleased to see us and interested in our mission. We'd like to think of him as a Rotary colleague, and so lobby him to explore Rotary membership.

After we get our rooms and secure our luggage, we gather briefly in the cocktail lounge with our hosts for introductions and orientation to our "Kano schedule." Dr. Owoka, who prefers to be called "Kola," tells us not to venture out alone. They (local Rotarians) will always accompany us. "You'll be safe when we are around." We nod, smile, and thank him, but do not truly appreciate the magnitude of what he has just said.

We gather the stubs from our plane tickets and give them to Kola as a basis of identification for our return flights. Privately, I give him the moneybag from Adefeso. He also takes some US dollars from each of us to exchange for the local currency we will need for meals, tips, and private shopping.

Our hosts have elected to take us first to the home and offices of Jonathan B. Majiyagbe. The house is vacant; J.B. and his wife Ade are in Evanston, Illinois. Mr. Majiyagbe is preparing to serve in 2003-04 as Rotary International's first African president. To the local Rotarians, his home and place of business at the same address already have the aura of a shrine. His up-coming presidency has brought special self-esteem to this community, evident in the pride of our hosts. Handsome 30-year old Majiyagbe son Jon gives us a tour.

Next in the line of protocol, we go to Dr. Owoka's Ideal Hospital, his privately owned and operated facility. His specialty is gynecology, but he has a young dentist and several other doctors and interns working for him. They work under challenging conditions and with limited resources.

Women in labor are pacing, trying to encourage their babies to enter the world. Rooms are small with a cot and a chair. A family member accompanies patients while they are hospitalized and attends to their needs. The hospital is very clean and the staff is caring and dedicated. Kola's staff obviously holds him in high esteem.

Dr. Kola was the Rotary District 9120 governor a year ago, a commitment surely requiring large blocks of time away from his business, and evidence of the competence of his staff and the mutual trust that he places in them.

It's gotten dark and we return to the airport to meet Ade Adefeso when he comes. We visit in the large parking lot of the airport with Joe, a Rotarian from Lagos. He will be going on to another northern state to work as a consultant and independent monitor during the NIDs.

We get acquainted with Amaka, an attractive young clinical psychologist and Rotarian who accompanies us. Electricity goes off and comes on several times. A crescent moon has risen. It's a quiet and pleasant evening on the West African savannah.

I find out that Randle Anthony, one of the Rotarians whom we met earlier, works for an international freight handler. Hmmm, maybe he can help in shipping the baby incubators that are be-

*Fulfilling Our Promise: Rotarians Volunteer in Kano, Nigeria*

ing acquired from the USA through a Rotary Foundation Matching Grant. They are destined for Amadu Bello University Teaching Hospital in Kaduna, a city two and a half hours south of here. My Kaduna friend, Francis Gana, is working on the project.

When Adefeso arrives, Dr. Kola and his wife Stella host us all for a light dinner at their home. A plaque hangs in their living room, a cherished award given Kola by last year's R.I. President Richard King to distinguish him among R.I.'s 530 District Governors.

On the dark streets driving back to the hotel, we gain an insight into the special relationship between the Rotarians in Kano and the traffic cops. In this part of the world, few intersections have traffic lights, so major intersections require the service of a traffic cop. It is always dangerous work but especially so at night because the uniform is dark, making the officer difficult to see. One of the Rotary Clubs of Kano donated to the police department dozens of bright yellow reflecting vests with the Rotary wheel prominently displayed, front and back. When Rotarians approach an intersection where traffic is directed, they are recognized and given favorable passage.

Phil and I are lodged on the second floor, the women on ground level. Barb and Kristin have a suite off the short corridor from the cocktail lounge. Karien and Sharon have one of the small but clean and adequate rooms off the corridor below Phil and me.

After deciding who gets which bed and dividing up the space that is left, Sharon and Karien turn on the air conditioner. Fortunately, the unit is located on the wall opposite the switch. As the unit rumbles to life, its frame and cover fall off onto Karien's bed. They decide to leave the A/C off and open the window instead. Before getting settled, the women make a complete shambles of their room, collapsing the curtain rod in the shower and knocking the drapery rod off the wall. In the morning, they claim all this stuff "just happened." Yeah, right.

## November 9: Saturday

At 8:00 a.m. we take up team business at breakfast in the Calypso Restaurant, part of the hotel compound. How to dress? We decide the handsome yellow Rotary Foundation tee shirts from Barb will be our "team uniform." We'll wear them to all the Rotary meetings, and we'll wear the yellow aprons of the volunteers when we are on NID work in the field. That's a relief to me. I had counted on a yellow Rotary windbreaker being my dress coat, but in the Nigerian climate the windbreaker is a sauna.

At nine the Rotarians pick us up. We head northwest in a caravan including Kola, Ade, Randall, Tom Brown and a vehicle with the CARE film crew. Our destination is the City of Katsina, a few miles from the border with Niger. The highway is paved, but drivers frequently swerve across the centerline to avoid potholes. Dangerous.

We push: a hard, three-hour drive, crossing from Kano State into Katsina State at about the mid-point of the trip. The landscape is filled with classical African scenes, but there is no stopping for photos, except finally at the Kofar of Katsina, the city gate, an unmistakable photo op for a hand-walk. We make another stop at a store where IPDG Kola looks for "his" immediate past president of the Rotary Club of Katsina.

The "flag-off" (we'd call it a kick-off) ceremony in Katsina is well-along when we arrive. We are surprised. This is the *Na-*

*tional* Flag-Off Ceremony here in this obscure, dusty little city on the edge of the vast Sahara. Something big *is* happening here in the North; the NID strategic planners, Ade Adefeso in the thick of it, are enlisting the support of traditional leaders, focusing the bright lights of the world community *here*, on the hold-outs, the populations that have on the basis of past experience or religious grounds rejected, or resisted, past polio eradication efforts.

The governor of Katsina State and the Emir are among the honored guests. The Emir is the top traditional leader of Katsina. Red carpet is spread before them and seated on either side of the carpet, facing each other, are two rows of barefooted but elegantly turbaned and brilliantly robed chieftains.

The agenda is comprised of a half-day list of leaders, officials, entertainers, witnesses, and dignitaries. Women and men spectators are seated on opposite sides, children across the open space. It is a media event. Photographers and camera crews with light and sound equipment, including my teammates and Scott Thigpen's CARE crew move about freely among this throng of old and new Africa.

As team leader, I am invited to sit in the shaded gallery among the dignitaries. It feels unseemly to take pictures in my position. My outrageous roommate Phil covers the bases, his backpack making him look incredibly important. Many officials wear green and white polio vests, the colors of Nigeria's national flag, patriotic symbols for Nigerian nationalists. Rotarians, we among them, wear yellow vests, the prestigious mark of volunteers.

One segment of the ceremony includes Rotary PDG Ade Adefeso, chairman of the National Polio Plus Committee, presenting certificates and awards of US$1000 to each of five young widows. All their husbands were killed as a result of one tragic

*November 9*

head-on auto accident during the last NID round. They were all volunteers. Barb wonders if five were killed. Here among the Islamic people, a man may have several wives. It doesn't diminish the tragedy to the survivors that perhaps fewer than five died in the accident, but the particulars...?

Two families who have had children recently stricken with polio come forth with their crippled babies. Although we cannot understand Hausa, the language they speak, the mournful quality of their voices leaves no doubt about the pain they feel for their stricken children. A street drama promoting polio immunization is performed; musical groups beat their drums and sing "polio songs."

All the speakers at this NID flag-off are on the same page..."Every child has the right to be immunized; kick polio out of Nigeria forever," etc. No stone is left unturned. When the ceremony ends, aides to the minister of health appear with a vaccine box armed with chilled vaccine, children are dutifully lined up and the audience watches as the emir and the governor administer vaccine drops to them. We volunteers are solicited to administer drops.

We've heard that some here consider immunizations an imposition of the Europeans and Americans. These people associate immunizations with unpopular campaigns for family planning, and possibly even the deliberate spread of AIDS. We wonder if our involvement is of strategic value or just a politically correct courtesy. That we are received and placed on equal ground with the emir and the governor in administering drops is an enormous compliment to us, if not also a bold move by our hosts.

Now we race southwest on another 2 1/2 hour leg of our day trip. All the landscape is agrarian. Farming by hand looks like the only way. Plant, cultivate, harvest – all by hand. We see good-

**Drive by shooting**: *Gerard Dolan of the CARE film team caught in a drive-by shooting between Katsina and Funtua. Greg Pope in sunglasses.*

looking cattle and mixed crops of millet, corn, beans, yams, and, as we get into irrigated areas, we see cotton. Even cotton is handpicked, delivered to market in bags.

More than once, the vehicle with Scott Thigpen's CARE film crew overtakes us, Gerard filming us as they pass. The open windows and the scorching wind have given us a weathered look, the countryside makes a great backdrop, and we think at the moment, "This clip should surely make the cut in *The Global Race to Eradicate Polio.*"

Mid-afternoon, we arrive in the City of Funtua, still in Katsina State. Amina Lawal Kurami, 31, is a young mother who, under the strict Islamic law of the Sharia, has been convicted and sentenced to death-by-stoning for bearing a child out of wedlock. Sharia has been adopted as state law by about a dozen of Nigeria's northern states. Lawal's home is here in Funtua, and her case has actually touched our lives.

*November 9*

Her situation has created an international uproar, affecting plans for the approaching Miss World Pageant in Abuja, Nigeria's federal capital, and weighing heavily on Dave and Barb Groner's deliberations about the mix of men and women on our team, the Kano team. We contemplate that except for the chilling case of this unfortunate young mother, some of us would be somewhere else today. How this changes the effect of our team also changes the war on polio. Looking at the people in the streets of Funtua, one would be surprised if they even know that their city is on the radar screen of the international media. Notoriety has certainly not brought them prosperity.

The states within Nigeria are subdivided into Local Government Areas (LGAs), which are roughly equivalent to counties in the USA. The top political officer of an LGA is the chairman. Each LGA is further subdivided into districts, and within the districts there are wards. Village is a generic term like city. Just as a city may overlap several LGAs (Kano City overlaps 5 or 6), a village may or may not overlap several wards. Current political boundaries have been influenced and intertwined with the ebb and flow of power that has been going on here for hundreds of years.

In theory state governors have replaced the emirs of old, LGA chairmen have replaced madakis, district heads have replaced hakemis, and village/ward heads have replaced chiefs. But, in a place where power may be synonymous with survival, theory sometimes loses. We will be confounded through the week by references to the dual leadership system: government leaders versus "traditional leaders," special consideration being given to the latter. We will *not* meet the Governor of Kano State, but we *will* meet the Emir of Kano.

We enter a community center of an LGA and briefly witness the training of independent monitors – people who will be assigned to certain areas to do quality assurance on the immunization campaign. The training is characterized by video taping, pre-testing and post-testing. It's a rigorous exercise to assure that those who report on the immunization efforts completely understand local aspects of the NID: social mobilization, markings, paperwork, cold chain, and surveillance for acute flaccid paralysis. The system counts on these monitors to provide high quality feedback on the successes and failures.

We meet with the chairman of the LGA to make our presence known and give our best wishes. This is one way we will serve the campaign, assuring those in positions of influence that the world is anxiously watching and cheering for their success in eradicating polio.

At 5 p.m., we head back to Kano, 2 1/2 hours more, almost due east, the third leg of a triangular route that gives us the flavor of two principal states in northern Nigeria. The sun is setting and our driver is going at speeds we think unsafe and unnecessary. We think of the widowed mothers in Katsina and don't want Ade Adefeso visiting our homes with $1,000 awards from The Rotary Foundation.

A Kano Rotarian with us explains that our driver has been fasting all day. This probably means he is a Muslim, hungry and anxious to get home for dinner. We had thought nothing about it, but this handsome, mild mannered young man who is our driver also has a family and practices his convictions. When the sun is down, we think he can break his fast. And if he eats, maybe he will slow down. We offer water and a power bar, but he refuses. Then as if to be reassuring, Phil adds:

*Before we came to Nigeria, I visited with a couple who were here for several months on a mission building schools. They said the roads are dangerous at night; bandits put up roadblocks and prey on those traveling after dark.*

***Independent Monitor training***: *This training exercise occurred in the City of Funtua, Katsina State. These trainees become independent monitors, the quality assurance arm of the National Immunization Days campaign.*

He's suggesting our driver isn't just in a hurry to get home and eat, hungry from fasting all day; he's trying to avoid an international incident! The discussion continues:

*There are also police roadblocks, even in the daytime. We passed through some this morning on the way to Katsina. Whether or not they are officially sanctioned, machine-gun-armed officers pull vehicles over, especially commercials, exacting payments. They said, the more people in the van, the larger the fee—just what we needed to hear. We're loaded.*

*This morning, our hosts spoke a few words, one of them "Rotarians," and we passed without incident. The side of our van has large Rotary lettering on it too; maybe that helps. Let's talk about something else.*

We arrive safely back at our hotel in Kano at 7:30 p.m. Needing relief from the long, intense day, we eat dinner together and our hair comes down. I hope I am not blushing at the stories and conversation between my urologist travel mate and the four women, but I feel like I am.

As Phil and I are bedding down, the electricity goes off. The room is dark, but we soon hear the hotel generator crank and fire up. As the throw-switch is transferred to the generator, the lights come back on. "NEPA," we laugh, Nigeria Electric Power Authority, Never Expect Power Anytime. Soon, the lights go out again, but the generator is still running. Maybe public power is back? Sure enough, as the throw-switch is transferred to NEPA, the lights come on and the hotel generator shuts down, a routine to which we become accustomed.

We eventually catch on that when power goes off or comes on, it is the guard from the hotel gate who runs a short distance to the shop and starts or stops the generator and transfers the switch.

Through the week, scarce electrical power will show itself repeatedly as an issue for the NID: the cold chain depends on it to run refrigeration, night time report meetings for lights and A/C, computerized data bases, telecommunications, airports for the arrival of vaccine—far-reaching dependence on electricity. The Nigerians and their international consultants must approach the NIDs with a contingency plan for back-up power at every juncture.

## November 10: Sunday

**Sunlight kills germs.** After our 8:00 a.m. team breakfast, we gather in the TV lounge to co-mingle the prizes we have for the children: goodies to attract attention to the immunization efforts—toys, gum, balloons, stickers and more. But, we will not distribute them. Barb's experience on prior NIDs has revealed how disruptive prize-giving by volunteers can be to the serious work of locals. Dividing them into five more-or-less equal collections, we bag them, one each for the four Rotary Clubs of Kano and one for the Rotaractors. We'll challenge them to put the prizes to best use in the fight against polio.

At ten "Africa time," we go to the chairman's office of an LGA. We wonder if the offices are always open on Sunday. Maybe they're open on Sunday for the NID? Or, just for us? We didn't come here to have our pictures taken, but a film crew has followed us and we will accommodate them, and any others. We are prepared to make little speeches and exchange friendly greetings.

But, something seems amiss. Tension hangs in the air. This gathering is much too auspicious to be explained by our visit. We begin to sense that we *might not be* the center of attention. Big vehicles pulling into the parking lot are marked World Health Organization, UNICEF, etc. In addition to the CARE film crew who is with us, and the R.I. photographer Jean-Marc, there is a television crew from Denmark. Denmark, a small country, is one whose government is a noteworthy partner in funding the international effort to eradicate polio.

After we, and many others, are crowded into the chairman's office, a man in faded blue jeans, western style shirt, and speaking clear English starts the meeting with the briefest of notice.

"Well, ladies and gentlemen, what we have to deal with here this morning is some sort of problem that has arisen..." With a diverse international audience present, cameras rolling and the world listening, the lead speaker, who is not the LGA chairman, goes on to explain, "For some reason, this LGA has had a mass exodus of the trained independent monitors. The untrained people who have replaced them cannot perform the necessary functions."

It appears that a local official has attempted to give the paying jobs of the NID to his people: wives, kids, neighbors' kids, political supporters, whoever. The particulars are never revealed to us, but the immediate implications give us a sense of nausea. We had planned to go out immunizing in this LGA today. It won't happen. Will it take a day, two days, a week, to recruit and train new independent monitors? Will they take back the original trained workers? The first criterion for independent monitors is to be able to read and write.

A representative of the Cold Chain, custodians of the vaccine, says the cold chain is not prepared for a postponement of the NIDs. An underling of the LGA chairman pounces on this revelation and suggests that success of the polio eradication program will depend on more reliable electric power and better refrigeration. This is bold-faced bargaining, using the NID as his hostage. We are surprised that his point is ignored—benignly ignored!

A robed, eloquent, fine-featured and distinguished-looking young man who has been standing among us speaks, introducing himself as Rabiu, a representative of UNICEF. Courteously, but plainly and with a better choice of words than these, Rabiu says, "We have heard this before, we (UNICEF and others) are sick and tired of coming to Kano and running into this. How much longer? Please, sir, let us get down to business." The

*November 10*

dignified young speaker might be a Fulani, one of the prominent ethnic groups of northern Nigeria.

We North American volunteers came into this room to make the usual courtesy call on a local leader, to give brief statements about our mission. But this is a political situation beyond our immediate comprehension. Independently, we all judge the situation will be best served if we not speak unless spoken to. The man running the meeting is running the meeting! In the tenor of John Wayne, he grants the alleged claim that the LGA chairman was unaware of the mass dismissal and substitutions. In the same breath, he welcomes cooperation to resolve the crisis.

The national and international advocates for the NID work feverishly at setting the stage for recovery from this fiasco. Ade Adefeso is among those who speak. He notes that volunteers have come from North America at their own personal expense to assist in the NID. It doesn't go unnoticed that both North American and European television and print media are recording the event.

We are little comforted; we've come here to immunize children against polio. What will we do now? This, after weeks of preparation? How can it be put right overnight? We leave with a sense of angry frustration. What can volunteers do in the face of these circumstances? The success of the NID in this LGA seems headed for the toilet.

As we are returning to our vehicles, I ask PDG Ade Adefeso, chairman of the National Polio Plus Committee, "This interference—will somebody pay?" His answer brings me back to reality, "We don't try to establish blame. We don't try to punish anybody. We just try to solve problems and get the job done." Then he thoughtfully adds, "Your being here means a lot in these situations."

There are 774 LGAs in Nigeria, 44 of which are in Kano State. I try to imagine 43 more offices like the one we just came from. We visited an LGA office yesterday in Funtua, in the neighboring State of Katsina. The comparison gives me two points of reference. In the van, we share our concerns and fears about the extent of local officials giving NID jobs on the basis of cronyism as contrasted with competence.

Jean-Marc has witnessed the challenges of NIDs across the world. His comments have a reassuring aspect. He gives us an appreciation of how unusual it is that a local leader gets caught red-handed, turning the NID to personal or political gain. Jean-Marc could not overstate the beneficial impact of having the incident so well witnessed. The NID surveillance system not only detected the problem early, but NID officials are now acting on the information, bringing every available tool to bear on correcting it. We happen to be in the right place at the right time, available as a tool.

In Jean-Marc's mind, there is no doubt that the LGA chairman knew about the trained workers being replaced and that everyone else in the room knew that the chairman knew; the lie was exposed to the world. Catching this on film should provide one of the dramas in Scott Thigpen's documentary film. Jean-Marc predicts the story of this humiliated local leader will spread like wild fire to LGAs, villages, and wards across the country.

Events of the morning have added fuel to Jean-Marc's fire. The free-lance photojournalist has joined us today, taking on the likeness of a Rotary volunteer. But he's steaming with indignation about "Nigeria." His interest in Polio eradication dates back several years. He has traveled everywhere and has had some pictures published in Life magazine prior to its demise. Then someone in Rotary picked up on his interest and asked him to cover this round of NIDs in Nigeria.

*November 10*

He arrived in Kano ahead of us and was arrested taking pictures in a market. He called PDG Kola Owoka, who bailed him out, but was hassled a couple more times. Finally, today, he dons the yellow Rotary apron. It surprises him how much freer he is to take pictures while associated with Rotarians, but he's still steaming, "Nigeria is the most difficult place I've ever been."

We visit another LGA where things are going better. The immunizing teams are in the field, working as planned. We make an attempt to join the work in progress. It's not easy, they are scattered in the village and our search turns out to be more of a village tour and sojourn in the streets. We are scattered in a side street with our vehicles parked nearby. Throngs of black children with smiling faces surround several of us volunteers. They love to have their picture taken and we oblige.

But our white skin is a greater curiosity. They want to touch us, and we want to be touchable. Like the picture taking, I oblige, reaching out to the group near me to touch as many as possible. And—possibly a mistake. I soon have a small, but strong, black hand gripping each of the fingers and thumb of my right hand. They are grasping for my forearm, all pulling together, and I feel myself moving. I'm vulnerable—camera in one hand and bag around my neck. While visualizing the scene of the Lilliputians in *Gulliver's Travels*, I tell myself not to panic, but I must react.

As I forcibly yank my hand free I hear a car honk and a voice commanding, "Get in!" I obey without hesitation, slamming the car door and hoping not to smash a child's hand. The children surround the car and pound on it, not in any apparent hostility but certainly sensing the power in their numbers. Looking back for other members of the group, I cannot see but can only hope that everyone else is safely in a vehicle. The children move back as we start to roll. Our hosts were watching atten-

*Fulfilling Our Promise: Rotarians Volunteer in Kano, Nigeria*

**Faces of Tomorrow**: *Late model cars contrast with the ancient dusty streets. It can be seen in their faces; the young people want to be heard.*

tively over us. It turns out that everyone is safe, but now I understand how quickly an innocent situation can become dangerous.

As soon as I see PDG Adefeso, I ask about the man who commanded the dramatic a.m. meeting. Adefeso seems to be thinking the same thing. He and I are soon on our way, leaving the rest of the volunteers in the care of Kano Rotarians. They finally meet vaccinators and join them in their work.

"The man" turns out to be Dr Daniel Fussum from Ethiopia, the World Health Organization's Head of Supplemental Immunization Activities (SIA) within EPI structure in Nigeria. Dr Fussum explains that at Nigeria's invitation WHO has 80 international consultants, mostly Africans, in Nigeria to assist with all aspects of this NID. He has 54 of them concentrated in 14 "priority states" in northern Nigeria. Fussum is one of us, an international participant in the NID. But, he is special; I gained an inkling of his stature in the morning meeting.

His office is a temporary command center, set up in a local hotel, the Tahir Guest House. His room, marked outside the door with a paper sign "World Health Organization Secretariat," is equipped with a laptop computer, mainframe, keyboards, fax machines, copiers, etc. Outside the hotel sits a back-up generator and a van equipped with a satellite dish receiver.

He explains that immunizing teams are recruited and supervised by the NID network, i.e. the federal and state Ministries of Health. But the teams are directed from house to house by locally appointed guides. When things work according to plan, local leaders trust feedback from their appointees, and then become advocates for, and participants in, the success of the campaign for their village or ward.

On the other hand, NID planners assign independent monitors and surveillance teams, if possible, from outside the area in which they work, attempting to keep them above the provincial temptations of fudged reports. Their job is to objectively test and report on the system, assuring progress of the NID.

Everyone is expected to participate in *surveillance*, looking for new cases of acute flaccid paralysis, AFP. Confirming the existence and the identity of the wild polio strain depends on appropriate handling, prompt delivery, and accurate testing of fecal samples from victims of AFP. Doctor Phil, my travel mate, had hoped to visit the national surveillance laboratory where fecal samples from AFP victims are tested, but the nearest is at Maidugari, a city far to the east near Lake Chad. It won't be possible to go. I bait, but Dr. Fussum does not bite, on the suggestion that Maidugari does not seem centrally located, even for northern Nigeria.

When the World Health Organization selects a site for a surveillance lab, *safety* is a primary consideration: safety for the facility, for the equipment and for the lab personnel. Sources in the US speculate that Kano, Kaduna, Katsina, and other cities in Nigeria's north central corridor apparently failed the safety test. Fussum does not say this; he knows better. The leadership code among these NID pros is evident even when unspoken. "We just try to solve problems and get the job done. (We make do with what we have.)"

Other questions lead to an invitation to attend the evening report meeting at which key personnel share their findings with Dr. Fussum and other officials, including his international consultants, the federal minister of health, state commissioner of health, cold chain representatives, etc.

*Sunday, November 10, continues on page 61.*

# COLD CHAIN
*By Phil Wise, MD*

The oral polio vaccine (OPV) contains a weakened, but live virus. In the ambient temperatures of Nigeria, all above 50 degrees Fahrenheit, the OPV virus dies and becomes ineffective in eliciting an immune response. Thus, the vaccine must follow and live in a "cold chain" from production site to delivery in the children's mouths. Inasmuch as Nigeria is a tropical country with large areas lacking good roads, electricity, refrigeration and communications, the cold chain is a subject of our curiosity.

Chemists have devised an indicator for the condition of the OPV. They call it the vaccine vial monitor (VVM). When the vaccine is new, the VVM is a white square printed in the center of a gray circle on a strip of paper that wraps around each tiny vial of OPV. The same conditions of light and temperature that cause the vaccine to die cause the white square to darken.

When the square is lighter in color than the gray circle, the vaccine is considered alive. When the square becomes darker than the gray circle, the vaccine is considered dead and useless. Under conditions adverse to the survival of the OPV, the square in the center of the VVM changes from white to black at about the same rate that the vaccine dies.

We witness the mechanics of the cold chain as the week progresses, but an early overview might aid the reader grasp some of the NID's technical complexities. Vaccine is received in Nigeria at a National Cold Store in the federal capital of Abuja. We learn that the cold chain for Kano consists of:

1. National Cold Store in Abuja
2. A Zonal Cold Store servicing 7 northern states. It has a walk-in freezer which we visit in Kano City. Nigeria has a zonal cold store located in each of the six geopolitical regions of the county.
3. A state Cold Store in Kano City serving all of Kano State. We saw it in a quick stop one evening at Nasarawa Hospital. There was a locked "Vaccines Cold Room" and an assortment of chest freezers along an outdoor, but covered walkway. Recent wiring had been added to provide electrical service for the freezers—common old, household deep freezers.
4. A regional cold store that serves six LGAs in the Kano City area. The regional cold store has a few chest freezers.
5. LGA facilities vary—maybe one chest freezer and maybe not. They are probably just insulated ice chests.
6. Supervisor-level Styrofoam or similar type chests.
7. Individual vaccine boxes for immunizers.
8. Two drops in each child's mouth.

There is a large inventory of molded plastic vessels containing a mixture of water and alcohol, approximately a liter, maybe two, in each vessel. When the contents are frozen, the mold resembles a block of ice or an ice pack. When the contents are in liquid form the mold might be called a flat, rectangular bottle. The vessel is formed with wells in the plastic into which the vaccine vials conveniently fit.

For personnel running the Cold Chain, the day starts long before the first drops of vaccine are squeezed. The ice blocks are frozen or refrozen during the night and packed with the vaccine vials into large ice chests early in the morning, then distributed down the chain to the LGAs.

From there, the vials are divided and placed into the insulated individual vaccine boxes and given to the vaccinators who start their rounds somewhere around 8 A.M. After about four hours of vaccinations, the ice blocks start to lose their ability to keep the vials cold and the exercise is over for the day as far as the vaccinators are concerned. But all the unused vaccine vials need to be collected and returned to cold storage. The Styrofoam boxes are relieved of their ice bottles, stored and secured. The ice bottles (ice packs) must be returned to cold storage and refrozen during the night for recycling the next day.

The individual vaccine boxes are about one half cubic foot, made of Styrofoam. Most have on each side the familiar logo "Kick polio out of Nigeria" and a long over-the-shoulder carrying strap. They are packed in a particular way: first in the box is one of the ice blocks, fitting snugly across the bottom. Next, enough OPV vials are loaded to vaccinate the target population for the day. Each vial contains 40 drops, enough vaccine for twenty children. In house to house vaccinations, two to three vials would serve a vaccinator each day. On top of the vials goes another moulded plastic vessel of frozen solution. Then on top of all that goes the Styrofoam lid. During the exercise, all the vials but one are sandwiched between the two ice blocks. The vial in use is seated within a cleverly designed well on the top block.

Quality control sweeps are routinely in progress. Independent monitors visit the districts, randomly checking all aspects of "the exercise," including the integrity of the cold chain. They make note of successes and failures. Their observations will be a subject of the evening WHO debriefings. During the first days of the exercise, the debriefings last well into the early hours of the morning. Everything must come together—mobilization of the parents and children, live vaccine, and surveillance. Every link of the cold chain is critical.

## November 10: Sunday—Continued

At 4 p.m., the four Rotaract Clubs and one Interact Club of Kano host us at a multi-club meeting jammed with singing, fellowship, and peppy reports. An HIV/AIDS Massive Awareness Campaign is among the projects of the Rotaractors. They are passionate about HIV/AIDS awareness and lobby us with brochures for financial support. We knew, coming here, that big problems compete with polio for attention and resources, HIV/AIDS among them. Here it is, in-our-face, at our first meeting.

Nonetheless, we feel affection and admiration for the Rotaractors, proud to acknowledge them as young Rotary associates. It is a bold new phenomenon in Africa to publicly acknowledge the existence and extent of HIV infection and AIDS. Rotaractor Bidemi Abidemi, who chairs the project, tells me the young people of Nigeria have been awakened. A former federal minister of health, Professor Olikoye Ransome Kuti disclosed that AIDS killed his brother, a popular Afro-beat musician Abamieda fela Anikulakupo Kuti. Nigerian media reported:

*The irony is that Fela himself saw AIDS as a "whiteman's disease." Apparently he was among many Nigerians who were under the impression that there is something about being African that gives you immunity.*

Touched by their objectives, but without forgetting that our mission here is polio eradication, we kindly wish our new young friends the greatest possible success in their project. Tomorrow we must, and we will, put on the Kick Polio Out of Nigeria aprons, walk on our hands, and keep as much attention as possible focused on the eradication of polio.

The Rotaractors' show of appreciation makes us feel eminently successful in our choice of prizes and used clothing for the children.  A young man gives each of us a bracelet, gifts from the Interactors.  Phil and I receive a different style than do the women.Barbara is humored when she is t old the bead-type bracelets given to the women are chief's bracelets and symbolize much power. The Rotaractor president presents broad-brimmed straw hats to each of us, including enough for the CARE film crew and Jean-Marc Giboux.

When the business meeting is done, the Rotaractors sing the Nigerian anthem and thoughtfully invite us to sing ours, at first not realizing that we represent two countries.  Being the only Canadian, the spotlight eventually falls on Sharon for her national anthem.  For the embarrassment that she endures, she becomes the darling of the meeting, raising a considerable sum in the auction of a charming woven basket, ultimately purchased and presented to her with great charisma by Randle Anthony.

A district Rotaract representative is present from Kaduna.  He sits on the left side of the room next to Mohamad I. Rahi.  The latter was president in the Rotary Club of Bompai the year Francis Gana and I were district governors.  Ideally, a special bond forms between district governors and their club presidents.  Mohamad and Francis enjoyed that bond, marching together in 1993-94 to the beat of RI President Bob Barth's drum: "Believe In What You Do, and Do What You Believe In." It's like old home week when Mohamad learns that Francis and I are personal acquaintances, for he recognizes that I too marched to that drum.

When the meeting adjourns, the district Rotaract representative invites me to Kaduna to visit my governor classmate Francis Gana and return tomorrow.  I have looked forward to seeing Francis; our relationship even played into the Groner's decision

***Rotaractors surround Sharon****: Warmth and hospitality of the young Rotaractors is evident as they surround Sharon from Canada at their multi-club meeting to honor the visiting North American Volunteers.*

that I should be on the Kano team. But I'm reluctant; once out of Kano, I'll be at a loss to control my schedule. And, as team leader, I have plans and obligations here. It is too early in the week to abandon the schedule. Expecting that I might go later, I decline, and I never make it to see Francis and Winnie.

For Christians, this day is a Sunday, and for Muslims this day is in the period of Ramadan, a time of all-day fasting. In the afternoon, the Muslims are hungry and thirsty, not very productive, and not always amiable. In deference to the Muslims, who break their fast only after sundown, the end-of-day WHO report meeting that I have been invited to attend will start at 8:00 p.m., allowing the Muslims time to eat before the meeting.

Adefeso and I arrive at 8:30. The meeting is underway. On one side of a long oval table sit about 25 district coordinators or supervisors representing several LGAs. On the other side sit several central facilitators, the international consultants, state and federal officials, WHO, UNICEF, and Rotary representatives. About half the people around the table are women. One by one, the locals give their reports. They are questioned, receive praise, criticism, and constructive advice. In some cases, the polio partners are already acting upon information that has been gathered. In other cases, action will be taken during the night or first thing in the morning.

What were today's problems?
1) Children who were represented as immunized were found not marked with the indelible Gentian Violet (GV) ink. It is said some teams did not have GV with them, to which is asked, "Did you look in their vaccine box?" It is said some mothers would present their children for the drops of vaccine, but in fear of their husband's reaction would ask that their children not be marked.
2) There was a fight in one locale, some thug belligerently insisting, "We don't need vaccine, we need clean water, give us clean water, give us electricity." The trouble-maker claimed polio could not spread in his community, "To spread, it needs water." The locals seem to know the person in question, an aspiring politician. (Phil will tell me later when he hears this story that he and Sharon actually witnessed it.)

3) Yesterday, some teams encountered rejection rates of 60 to 90%. Homes where rejection occurred were marked and recorded by the independent monitor. They were reported to the village leaders. Local leaders have started talking to the husbands. Today, it was common to go back and immunize almost all those who refused yesterday. The campaign wants to establish quickly that local leaders will not be content with households where the vac-

cine is rejected. Word seems to get around, evidenced by a somewhat lower rate of rejection reported today. Jobs and services could hang in the balance, and husbands do not want to be on the wrong side of their local leaders.

4) It's discouraging for immunizers to keep going in the face of rejection. Keeping morale up is a constant challenge. That some vaccinators went about today's work singing merits a favorable remark in their supervisor's daily report. But the superviser's view does not meet with universal acceptance: a strong woman seated along the wall reminds the group that this exercise is not work to be taken lightly.

I detect a nuance in the language of the house-to-house NID. Resistance does not mean rejection. **Resistance** means the household *at first* refuses. **Rejection** means the *final* answer is "no," even after the village head talks to the husband.

The central facilitators recite one little drama after another: unqualified eight and nine year olds discovered working as vaccinators and independent monitors, not knowing any of the right answers; home workers not showing up for work, being dismissed, and replaced; immunizers caught "going out to the hills" with water (as opposed to ice) in their boxes. Their vaccine would die, if it had not already. The exercise was stopped and started over.

As the central facilitators tell their stories, the leader of the meeting, time and again, implores and commands them, "Please stick to the format of the questionnaire!" Representatives of the cold chain have complaints about demands on them. Counter complaints are revealed about the services of the cold chain. Houses were found to be incorrectly marked. Why?

Most leaders exercise a good deal of patience and tactfulness in addressing problems. One exception is a large woman wearing a gold cross necklace. She aggressively questions each report, frequently praising, but sometimes badgering and harassing the witness. She makes her presence known and her influence felt. I have the impression that she is the federal minister of health. She will move on to another city tomorrow, but not before interfering with the work of Scott Thigpen's film crew.

I try to look through the toughness of this fire-breathing "Dragon Lady." She has a job. She is courageously doing it, and who can measure the value of passion and leadership from a woman in this land and in this war? As the federal minister of health, she is the gate-keeper, letting the international community into Nigeria, perhaps inviting them in, as we had been invited, to assist with the NID. Perhaps she reports to the President. She seems to reflect impatience and embarrassment that Nigeria has been slow to eradicate polio, and even fear that Nigeria could fail. Perhaps Nigeria's place in the history of polio is on her shoulders. She can be loving, compassionate, and constructive as well as impatient and acidic, a woman wearing a large gold cross close to her heart, marking herself as a Christian.

Adefeso and I leave after a couple of hours. These nightly report meetings have a reputation of going into the wee hours. It is encouraging, before we leave, to pick up an emerging generalization; "What you saw yesterday, the first day of the NIDs, is not what you saw today; problems are fewer and work is more productive. Today vaccinators were singing."

Back in the room at the Prince Hotel, I tell Phil about the WHO report meeting. He's astonished when he hears about the confrontation in the village. He wonders if it was the "close call" that his team encountered earlier in the day while Adefeso and

I were meeting Dr. Fussum, and apparently it was. The house guide must have reported it to his supervisor, who reported it to the central facilitator, who reported it at the evening WHO meeting. Phil's first hand account:

*Sharon, Jean-Marc and I meet a vaccinator and her house guide at the place where they hand out the vaccines. The house guide is around 20, left home about a year ago, but grew up in this neighborhood. He knows the streets and alleys and where all the children live. After about a ten-minute walk, we are going down a dirt street when I become aware that a clean, late model sedan has stopped behind us. The dirt street we are on is a dead end. We had just turned in ahead of the car, and it now blocks our path of retreat.*

*In a way that spells trouble, four well-dressed men get out of the car. The driver obviously is their leader. He says that he doesn't want any one in his neighbourhood vaccinated—what they need is water and power. Our house guide politely inquires if there are any children to vaccinate. Jean-Marc starts arguing, and I am concerned that this might turn ugly. Our French photojournalist asks how can they turn down free vaccine? How can he sentence the children in his area to the crippling effects of polio when they could be protected?*

*The leader raises his voice and starts walking toward us, shouting that what they really need is power and water. I'm beginning to think tactics. Are these guys armed? If not, I might take out the two on the right. Can Jean-Marc handle the one in the middle? What about our house guide? The street-wise vaccinator has taken Sharon and left. And then what I witness is the value of a local street guide. He starts by cooling Jean-Marc down, letting him know that the leader has a reputation as a troublemaker and that the district head will deal with him. The leader and his henchmen head for a doorway, and we go our way.*

*About the time we catch up with Sharon and the vaccinator, she stops and buys a bolt of fabric from a vendor in the street.*

Phil says he would have just as soon kept going. I sleep restlessly, processing my day's education.

## November 11: Monday

At four o'clock, I decide to get up and write. I can sit in the bathroom where the light won't bother Phil. Then the power goes out. I sit in the dark bathroom for a couple of minutes. When the hotel generator starts, it wakes Phil. He notices light coming under the bathroom door; he can see in the dim light that I am not in my bed. He's afraid I have one of the two dreaded travel problems. At six, awakened again, he sees the light still on in the bathroom and me not in my bed. He thinks, "Oh God, Norm is going to have all my good toilet paper used up." He's a very sympathetic doctor.

At breakfast, Kristin is dehydrated and can't take even water. She *has* had a bad night, spending a lot of time in the john. She blames it on food she had for dinner. We inventory our "pharmacies"—we have enough drugs to open a store—and come up with re-hydration salts. Stirred into solution, they settle her stomach and she joins us for the day without a hiccup in the schedule, and thankfully, not on the trail.

As we are all getting into the van, I bait Sharon: "Phil says you were oblivious to the incident yesterday in the village." She takes the bait, and as if Phil had said it to her directly, she rejoins the account.

"I wasn't *oblivious*, Phil. I saw and heard what happened. I knew that I wouldn't be of any help to you so I got out of the way."

***House guides wait***: *Because men may not enter, these house guides wait while the women vaccinators are inside a home. Guides record the result after each house call.*

The Rotarians of the main Kano club take us to meet the Commissioner of Health for Kano State. He's not in. We go to a district office in one of the LGAs. Immunizers have been at work and some are called in so that we can join them. They are already tired, but agree to go back out so we can witness the work.

For my first time, I walk with teams from block to block, house to house. All the immunizers are women. Men cannot go into another man's home when he is not there. Among our teams, however, the independent monitors are men; they do the paperwork for each stop. With chalk they mark the home above or beside the door with a code that signifies the result of the visit.

Block to block, house to house, the process is slow and tiring

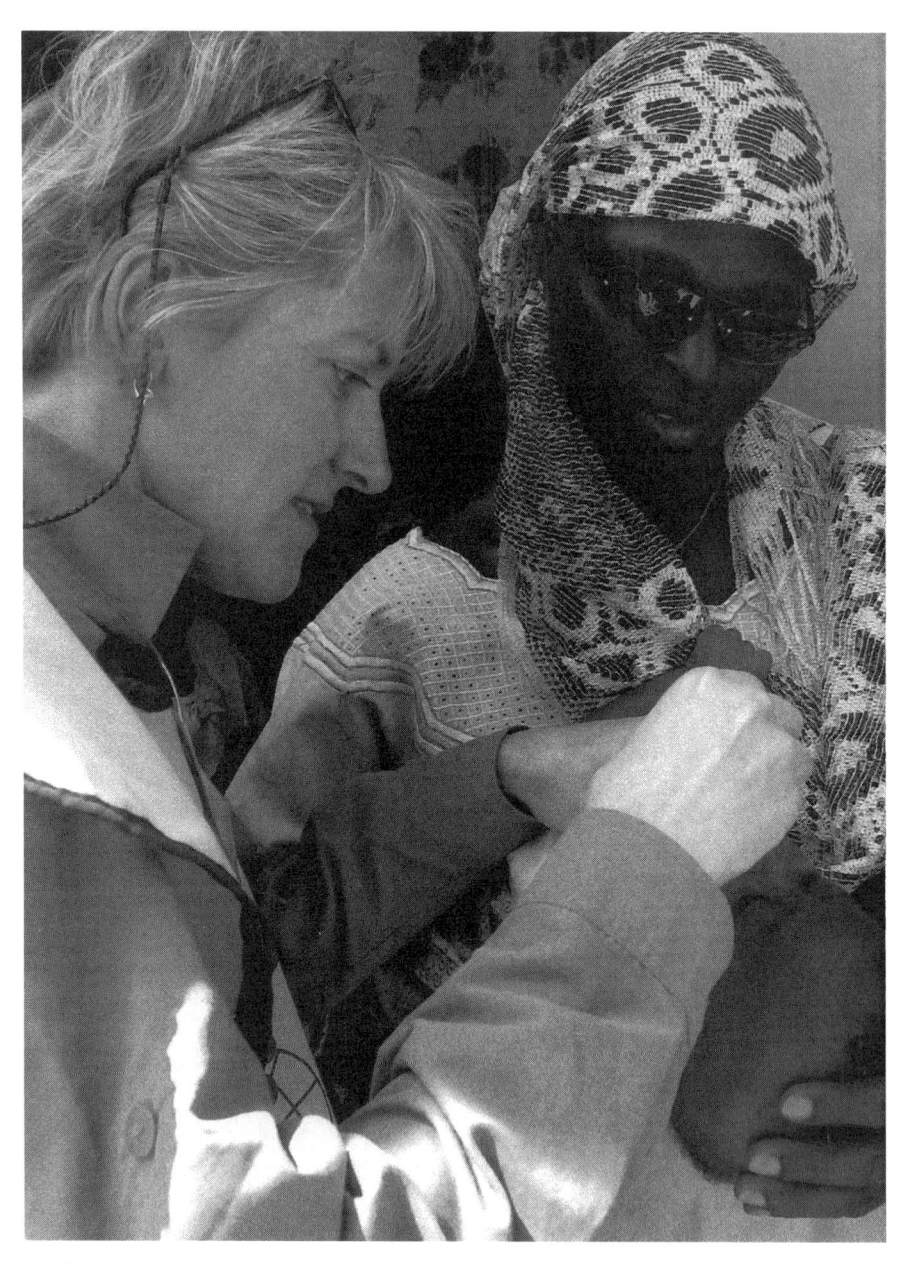

*Fulfilling Our Promise: Rotarians Volunteer in Kano, Nigeria*

**Kris gives vaccine**: *Rotarian Kris from Wisconsin, USA and Rotarian Joy from Abuja, Nigeria give drops of oral polio vaccine to a child of an Islamic home in Kano.*

but methodical and steady. We add nothing to the productivity. We surely slow them down, but the teams are patient and friendly with us. Perhaps our interest gives a meaningful additional dimension to their work; it boosts their esteem. It seems to be so for the Rotarian nurse Joy from Abuja who has come to serve in Kano as a team supervisor and is supervising the teams we follow. We are her peers, Rotarians who left our homes to lend our support here in Kano.

We will be attending an evening Rotary meeting, which will not include dinner. So we eat early and go to the market across from the Central Hotel. Each of the four Rotary clubs of Kano meets at the hotel on a different night of the week. The market enjoys an ideal location for tourists from the hotel. It features semi-precious stones, bone carvings, handcrafted leather products from Kano's famous tanning industry: skins of kid goats, large snakes, cattle, etc. I like the offerings in wood and pick out some traditional carvings in ebony and teak.

Prices are high, but negotiable. Twenty-six year old Kano Rotarian Tom Brown has accompanied us and offers to represent us in negotiations. We pick out what we might want to buy and he will "settle" the prices. We have no idea what prices are fair and Tom's help takes our ignorance factor out of the equation.

As eight o'clock approaches, we leave our selections for Tom's negotiations and cross the dark and dangerously busy street to attend the weekly meeting of the Rotary Club of Kano, the home club of Jonathan B. Magiyagbe, Rotary International President Elect. The same Tom Brown who helped us at the market across the street is the club secretary for Kano. He is a bright lawyer and works for J. B. Majiyagbe. Tom is articulate and critical of the traditional ways in Nigeria, including "mumbo jumbo" Rotary protocol.

They tell us the Rotary Club of Kano, chartered in 1961, was the first Rotary Club in Nigeria. We are seated at the head table and introduced almost immediately. A past district governor speaks on The Rotary Foundation. True to form, a dry presentation, but a good prelude to a fundraising hand-walk. I go to another part of the room, out of sight and stretch.

When the time comes, Barbara explains the fundraising aspect of my hand-walking. To illustrate how it works, Phil offers to pay 5 naira for each step of this particular hand-walk. Others catch on and begin matching him. Finally, there's a "democratic" rush to agreement; they'll all pay 5 naira per step. It's an 81-step walk. The treasurer collects 400 naira from everyone, and when the money is all counted, 20,000 naira have been donated for the Rotary Foundation, about $150. Tom tells me later that in his memory it is the second largest fundraiser the club has ever had for the Rotary Foundation.

After we present the children's prizes and used clothing, the president allows that we should close the meeting with the singing of *Oh Canada* and *The Star Spangled Banner*, no accompaniment, thank you. Sharon, having watched enough hockey games, knows the American anthem and sings heartily with us. For the Canadian anthem, the American volunteers lipsync, trying hard so Sharon doesn't have to go it alone. It's coming.

Phil and I sit up late visiting with Tom Brown at a table in the courtyard. Tom briefs us on what to expect in the morning at the Emir's palace. A yellow first quarter of the moon pierces through a high thin layer of clouds. Here, near the equator at this time year, the first quarter appears as a round-bottomed cup, the top parallel to the horizon.

Tom speaks almost reverentially of the Emir as a compassionate and progressive leader, very supportive of the Polio Plus campaign, a friend of Rotary. A story circulates that one of his ministers, living in the palace compound with his family, publicly stated his opposition to the polio vaccine, saying that it is a means by which foreigners will sterilize Nigerian children, even that it contributes to the spread of AIDS. As the story goes, the Emir was so angered by this that he banished the man and his family from the palace, and then to show that he trusts the vaccine, he personally and publicly immunized those of his many children who were young enough to receive the vaccine.

The luminescent half-disk of the moon descends in the western sky. As we part, Tom, alluding to the casual departure times of previous days, tells us to be ready on time, "The Emir does not observe 'Africa time.'"

I dream restlessly of addressing the Emir, hearing the hotel generator cycle on and off a couple of times during the night, a reminder of the meaning in the initials N.E.P.A.

## November 12: Tuesday

**The day we visit the Emir.** We are ready and leave promptly at nine o'clock with the children's clothing in the colorful bag, custom-made by my fourth sister, Colleen Fryer. Dr. Kola Owoka is our guide and leader. Our delegation is large, many local Rotarians accompanying us, perhaps on the chance that they will be included in the audience with the Emir. Their presence is reassuring, a clear showing of interest and support for our visit to Kano, *and* a strong statement of Rotary's internationality. Perhaps J.B. Majiyagbe counselled his fellow Rotarians about our visit before he left for Evanston?

Under the former theocratic states that functioned in northern

Nigeria, emirs were the chief executives of government in their respective emirates, the commanders-in-chief. Under the Nigerian constitution emirs have no official governmental authority. But Emir Ado of Kano has played his cards well, maintaining a powerful public position through his successful business ventures and the careful choice of issues on which he speaks.

The audience with Emir Ado will be a privilege of gigantic proportions. He is one of the richest and most influential men in Nigeria, respected for his wealth and revered as a spiritual leader among the Muslim masses of the North. He is age 71, and although he does not converse with visitors, Tom Brown told us, "He speaks the Queen's English." In the early years of Nigeria's independence, he served in the Nigerian diplomatic corps. He still travels widely, visiting the USA almost annually.

Emir Ado is no doubt informed and, one might speculate, as proud as any other citizen of Kano, about the up-coming presidency of his local contemporary J.B. Magiyagbe in the worldwide fellowship of Rotary. In this vein, one might also wonder if a combination of friendship between the Emir and Magiyagbe, along with Magiyagbe's presidency of RI, might be the seedbed for extending Rotary fellowship to more of the Islamic World. Is this ancient and obscure City of Kano on the edge of the Sahara Desert prepared for a role in the history of Rotary International?

Up to a point, everything unfolds just as Tom Brown described it. After entering the palace gate, we disembark from the van and walk through a long marbled courtyard where criers sing praises of the Emir. Then comes a large vestibule-like room where we leave our shoes and where men sit reading the Koran aloud as we walk between them. Next we pass through an archway and enter a domed waiting room, elaborately painted in traditional designs. Some parts of this palace date back 700 years.

*November 12*

**Waiting room of palace**: *Sharon and Karien, wearing scarves in the Islamic custom of modesty, sit among host Rotarians in the waiting room of the ancient palace of the Emir of Kano.*

Could this have once been the throne room? What secrets does it harbor?

We sit in the splendor of the ancient room for a period of time and visit with our Rotarian hosts. The latter seem at ease; Randle Anthony pays me a compliment attempting to walk on his hands. As the conversation becomes loud, Kola urges everyone to quiet down in respect for the readings in the next room.

On one side of me sits the young woman who was introduced at last night's club meeting as a visiting Rotarian from Abuja. Her name is Joy, and I finally realize that she is the bright, steady, hardworking nurse who is in Kano as a participant in the polio

NID. She was the supervisor directing the teams of vaccinators we followed from block to block yesterday in the village. I ask her how it is that she is not in the village today. She says there are other supervisors who rotate in the schedule. When the professional photographer comes by, I put my arm around Joy's shoulder and squeeze her.

We fall in love, and I give her a pin from my home Rotary Club of Elk Rapids. Later, when prints of our photograph come out, she will present one to me. We have good intentions of autographing and writing some endearing message each on the other's print, but something happens on the way to Kano and the promises are not kept—moments of honesty and nets of safety that surround people-to-people aspects of Rotary exchanges.

On the other side of me sits a Rotarian who owns rigs for doing boreholes. I ask about the hydrology of Nigeria. It sounds like water will normally come in at 150 to 200 feet. As he begins to explain the fascinating differences between different regions of the country, Kola commandingly announces, "Come, come, the Emir will receive us now."

We are taken through another courtyard where guards are present and into the presence of the Emir in the throne room. We are wearing our yellow polio tee shirts and baseball-style, bright yellow polio caps. It seems a dreadful paradox in decorum as we know it –we have taken off our shoes, but we don't take off our hats? In fact, the women have thoughtfully worn scarves to cover their heads in the Islamic custom of modesty.

Soon the Emir appears before us in dark glasses, a white robe, lower face covered with an emerald-colored scarf tied up around his head, like the photo we had found of him on the Internet. He shakes each of our hands, including those of the women.

The only protocol we knew in advance for the women was to wear scarves. We didn't know who would be expected to speak. The Emir is hidden from our view by a temporary curtain as he seats himself, and then we are invited to seat ourselves in the chairs along the side of the room to the Emir's right.

When everyone is settled, Dr. Kola takes the initiative. He prostrates himself before Emir Ado and then rising explains that the Rotarian volunteers who have come from the United States of America and Canada wish to address His Royal Highness and make a presentation. It is definitely an introduction that sets the stage for each volunteer to speak. This is the first clue that each of the team members might speak for him/herself.

Kola introduces me as the team leader, indicating that I will make further introductions. The ball is in my court. One of our host Rotarians has carried in the brightly colored bag of used clothing and placed it three paces in front of the Emir. Between the Emir and the bag, a sword lies on the floor. Advancing, I look down and remember clearly, "Don't approach the Emir closer than the line marked by the sword that lies across the floor in front of him." In the marking out of space, it appears that ours has been defined by the location of the bag. I stop beside it.

Tom had told us prostrating is not necessary for everyone, but a very shallow genuflection with left fist raised (or was it right fist?) would be considered a courteous gesture. A stir comes from the back of the room as I stop and execute the movement. I know not whether it is a sign of surprised approval, amusement, or embarrassment to our hosts at some unknown gaff.

I begin, "His Royal Highness, Emir of Kano, Alhaji Dr. Ado Bayero, ladies and gentlemen, my name is Norm Veliquette. I am from the state of Michigan in the United States of America.

*Fulfilling Our Promise: Rotarians Volunteer in Kano, Nigeria*

***Emir Ado****: Emir of Kano, His Highness Alhaje Ado Bayero, addresses the Rotarian delegation in Hausa language through an interpreter. Emir Ado's outspoken support for the campaign to eradicate polio is a critical factor in overcoming resistance to the vaccine in Nigeria's Islamic North.*

It was the organization of Rotary that brought me together with my volunteer teammates, and it is the crippling disease of polio that brings us to Nigeria and to Kano. We are here to lend our physical presence and moral support to the efforts in Nigeria to eradicate the crippling disease of polio. We know that His Highness has provided leadership in the polio eradication campaign, and that he has participated in the immunizations." That said, I know that our visit should be brief and I will not waste the Emir's time by repeating myself.

Although they have not been asked to prepare, I will introduce my teammates. I am confident in their abilities. I have heard them speak at the Rotary meetings; they are eloquent, each with details and personal testimony about the objectives of our mission. One by one they stand next to the bag, sincerely proclaiming our fellowship with the Nigerians as partners in the polio eradication campaign and expressing passion for the success of the effort.

When Sharon speaks as a Canadian, magic fills the room. We are no longer an *American* delegation; her identity makes us *North Americans.* We have accepted her, and she us. We dress alike, we speak in a common tongue and with a single message. It is a statement of internationality that cannot be missed. We represent a large community from the outside world, and the presence of our local Rotary counterparts makes us one with the Nigerians. It makes me feel taller to be here today!

In the manner that I have adopted for introducing Barbara, I tell the Emir that our gifts are of a nature that is appropriately presented only by a mother and a grandmother. Barb goes beside the bag and explains that we have brought children's clothing that His Highness may distribute to those in need.

Throughout Kola's and our presentations Emir Ado has nodded his understanding and his approval, but has not spoken. When we finish our presentations, he speaks. Sticking to custom, he addresses us through an interpreter in Hausa, the native language of northern Nigeria. He thanks us for our gifts of clothing, for our support in the National Immunization Days campaign, and expresses his hope for continued international support. We pick up phrases in his reply that we have used in addressing him, notably "the crippling disease of polio." We know that we have communicated. Finally, he gives us his blessing and best wishes for safe travel.

Court photographers line us up in the sunlight outside the door and Emir Ado comes and stands in the center for photographs. Barbara and I with Karien stand at his left; Sharon, Kristin and Phil to his right, our Rotarian hosts farther out on both sides.

*Fulfilling Our Promise: Rotarians Volunteer in Kano, Nigeria*

**Group photo with Emir of Kano**: *Local and International Rotary Volunteers are privileged in an audience with His Highness, the Emir of Kano; North American volunteers stand to his immediate left and right.*

*Norm's handwalk in front of the Emir's palace*

When the photo shoot is finished, I make eye contact with him through his dark glasses. With appreciative smiles several chime in, "Thank you, Your Highness." He smiles, again nodding acknowledgment.

On the way out, there is a din of conversation and people moving about in the large outside courtyard. I hand-walk. As I start, sharp shouts ring out. Perhaps they are commands to me. Perhaps hand-walking is inappropriate here. I am disgusted with my temerity in not explaining my personal quest to Emir Ado, allowing him, if he should have liked, to suggest a hand-walk in the inner courtyard. One huge opportunity has slipped away; this time I will keep going.

Phil is supposed to be videoing, and I will make this worthwhile. A hush falls over the courtyard. The shouts have apparently attracted everyone's attention to the hand-walker. Will I be surrounded by men with guns when I finish? Then people begin to laugh with amusement. Unknown to me, one of the robed locals is following me on all fours, robe spread out like a gigantic bug. He is the object of the laughter, and when I stand up I see him – a funny guy, a real sport. He upstaged me, rather unusual that this should happen. He wouldn't have dared if the Emir had been watching!

After a quick change into work clothes at the hotel, we go to the Wakilin Arewa District, one of eleven in the Dala LGA. Dala is said to be the largest LGA in all of Nigeria's 774 LGAs, probably measured by population. The central facilitator is Mrs. Poline Kaigama. She is clear and confident in the numbers for her organization: 302 immunization teams, 50 team supervisors, and 12 independent monitors, working all 11 districts of the LGA.

She makes clear that her 50 supervisors include the personnel known also as district coordinators, district supervisors and state supervisors. How has it happened that this administrative giant has been placed here, at the core of Nigeria's challenging north? As she speaks, our hopes soar that there are others like her in other LGAs.

We take a brief tour of a nearby village. It's an old part of Kano, real old. The crooked street leading into the village is extremely narrow, barely a pathway on each side of an open gutter. We go single file on one side of the sewer as we meet pedestrians going the opposite direction on the other. Outside one particular domicile, a group of men, young and old, sit crowded in a deeply social attitude. It's a scene to capture the imagination of every photographer. We've learned to ask permission for photographs, usually being granted approval, but this time the answer is "no." After we clear the next corner, the locals with us speculate that the scene we had just passed is a wake. Someone in the household perhaps had just died, or is near death. In their grief, the family and friends would not want to be photographed, of course.

The sweep team with whom we are walking reaches a residential area where the street is wider, but in the center is the open sewer, clogged with plastic trash and excrement. Our women teammates enter a house with the vaccinators, leaving us men in the street. Phil and I are white, dressed in yellow aprons and loaded with our gear. Phil is on one side of the sewer, I am on the other. We both take pictures, each attracting growing crowds of youngsters. Time wears on as we wait for the vaccinators to emerge. For the youngsters, curiosity over these "whites" leads to familiarity. They like having their pictures taken.

I've become a little street smart and recognize this as a hand-walking opportunity with multiple possibilities. Getting ready to hand-walk creates some suspense, buying time as I tuck my apron into my belt, take off my glasses, give my camera bag to

*November 12*

***Phil attracts a crowd***: *Phil's ability to show young people their images on the screen of his digital camera was a great source of entertainment. Wakilin Arewa District, Dala LGA.*

Phil, stretch my body and put on my leather gloves. The actual hand-walk invariably provokes admiration among the young men and boys in the audience. They become my pals, our protectors, buying us an enormous measure of credibility and goodwill.

But this is a place for a hand-walk that has something more, lots more. After enjoying the recognition of hand-walking in India with a pristine reflecting pool in front of me and the Taj Mahal with its wealthy tourists behind me, I have an obligation to hand-walk here, an obligation to myself, to the ideal that there is merit in hand-walking to promote the eradication of polio.

I must hand-walk in Nigeria with an open sewer in front of me and the red brick abodes of Dala with their impoverished children behind me. Phil is in the right spot to get the whole pic-

*Fulfilling Our Promise: Rotarians Volunteer in Kano, Nigeria*

Norm's handwalk in front of the open sewer.

ture! This will never make the *Rotarian*, but it will have a spot in my memory and in my scrapbook of hand-walking photos next to the Taj Mahal.

We eventually return to Poline Kaigama's office to give our parting regards. Her teams are reporting in and are thrilled that today they have been allowed access to several Islamic schools where they immunized over 100 children in each. With obvious encouragement, Mrs. Kaigama uses the words "break through."

Then she takes us next door to the office of the District Chairman, Sayadi Muhammad Yola, an Islamic leader who loves all of his 23 children. He visits enthusiastically with us, to the point of wearing us down, about the possibility of wiping out polio. A showman, he dons a polio vest and hat for photos. He is obviously among the progressive leaders who play a critical role in gaining access to the children of suspicious Islamic parents.

In stopping to visit with Sayadi, we have again observed one of the strict rules of NIDs: "Traditional leaders are to be consulted and informed about everything that goes on in their neighborhood!" One gets the feeling that this rule might have been violated in previous NIDs, ignoring and perhaps alienating a vital level of support.

As the visit wears on, our vehicle returns and waits outside, blocking the street. Traffic comes to a standstill for as far as we can see in both directions and our hosts are visibly anxious. Other drivers are vocal in their displeasure. By the time we all get aboard, it's a situation with explosive potential. By some small miracle, a riot is averted. Vehicles begin to wiggle free like an ice-floe breaking up and we get out alive.

Phil and I wonder aloud to our women teammates, "What's it like inside the houses with the vaccinators?" Descriptions continue through dinner:

*You see the same brick and adobe materials inside that you see outside, earthen bricks formed from the red earth and baked in the hot sun, same as the walls that surround the villages. The building materials and designs cannot have changed much for centuries. But, there's evidence of change. On one street, we saw a new house under construction where the builders were using concrete blocks, mortar and reinforcing rod in the corners.*

*The neighborhoods we visited the first three days have been similar. A short hallway, or small room serves as an entry from the street to the courtyard. The entrance is designed with a corner to block the view from the street, giving privacy to domestic activity inside. Off one of the entrance hallways today, there was a set of narrow steps leading up to a metal door on the upper level, the husband's quarters where wives would go only when invited. The husband receives visitors just off the street, then invites them in or not as he chooses. We saw no furnishings or fixtures in these entrances.*

*Inside, the homes consist of several rooms surrounding an inner courtyard. Each wife has one of the rooms off the courtyard as a home for herself and her children. In Nigeria, it is claimed that there are three women for each man. So the practice of multiple wives is a practical way of addressing this population skew. (Do both the men and the women say that?)*

*One particular home that we entered seemed typical. It had two small rooms. One was a living room/dining room/all purpose room, and the other was a tiny bedroom for the whole family. The all-purpose room had a small breakfront cabinet, with seven sets of new ceramic pots, part of the woman's dowry, displayed on top of the unit. There was a small upright refrigerator in the corner, and overstuffed chairs and sofas on the room's perimeter.*

*The young mother in this home had a baby who was just recovering from a very serious illness, perhaps meningitis. She was gracious and welcoming. After we visited and asked to take her photo, she had to first cover her head; her husband would not want her picture taken without her hair covered. But, it was okay to leave her lovely face and smile open to the camera.*

*Barb witnessed two refusals. One mother said there were three children under five, but she could not let them be immunized without her husband's permission. The immunizer had the house guide make note of this on his sheet and chalk mark the house outside the door with a circle, R in the middle, and the number 3 just beside it, meaning 3 children refused vaccine. On another occasion the mother allowed us to give drops to the children, but not to mark their thumbs! There is a column on the record sheet for "Thumb marked."*

*One mother adamantly rejected the OPV. Her "NO" was emphatic, representing a lingering anger and distrust toward drug companies. In 1996 meningitis swept through Kano, killing thousands and leaving others permanently disabled. As the death-toll rose, state radio told families to take sick children as quickly as possible to the Infectious Diseases Hospital where the aid organization Medecins Sans Frontieres (MSF) was providing free emergency treatment.*

*What the radio did not say was that representatives of the drug company Pfizer were also at the hospital conducting tests on a powerful new drug, Trovan. Subsequent challenges to the safety of Trovan has fueled lawsuits in Nigeria against Pfizer, providing sensational grist for the Nigerian media. Deaths and disablement of children who were, or who were thought to be, involved in the tests have been blamed on the Trovan. Whatever is true, the controversy leaves mothers and fathers susceptible to believe that Trovan was bad, and the polio vaccine could be another ruse with insidious consequences.*

*Courtyards are communal areas. Women use this space for cooking, laundry, hanging clothes to dry, and caring for their children. Here where women are discouraged from being seen in public, they enjoy the company of the other wives in the household. They share chores, helping with each other's children. One woman described it as a "sisterhood." The walls of the inner courtyards define the space between households but are frequently low enough to allow socializing between the women of different households.*

*They cook in large pots over small wood or charcoal fires in the courtyard. Foods consist mainly of root vegetables, goat, and chicken. Hunger and starvation are not apparent at this time of year; the growing season has just ended and the abundance of the harvest is evident in the markets. Laundry is done in large plastic bowls and hung to dry over lines in the inner courtyards where the goats and chickens often wander.*

*Electricity does not seem uncommon, but fresh water does. Barb remembers a young boy, maybe ten or so, in one inner courtyard, at the well getting water. The "rope" he was using was made from pieces of fabric tied together. The well was a raised adobe stoop with an 18" hole, kept covered by a metal lid when not in use. Water is generally retrieved from a community well or purchased from vendors who wheel carts along, loaded with five-gallon plastic jugs. One source blamed much of the waste plastic in the environment on the practice of packaging and selling water in thin plastic bags.*

We learn that a cameraman in the back of the room this morning at the palace was from the local television station and that our visit to the Emir will be broadcast on both editions of the evening news, Hausa and English. After cleaning up and dressing for the evening, we eat early and then wait anxiously in the TV lounge. To no avail. The hotel TV does not carry the local

*November 12*

***Butcher****: In the absence of refrigeration, food preparation is an ongoing function. There might be a source of fresh meat in the shade of the closest tree.*

news—CNN and European counterparts. But not local.

As we reconcile ourselves to the disappointment, it dawns on us, our presence has again served as a tool, this time for Emir Ado of Kano to go on television and make a definitive statement in favor of the immunization campaign, the safety of the vaccine. Who cares if we are on TV? As for the Emir, his position will not go unnoticed by leaders at any level in the Islamic North. This is social mobilization at its best, and Y3K is at the forefront, at the highest levels of regional society. This is what we came here to do. When Segun arrives, we ask if he might get a copy for us of the broadcast video.

Dressed again in our team uniforms, bright yellow polio baseball hats and blue-collared yellow tee shirts, we attend the meeting of the Rotary Club of Tarauni-Kano. Our routine has fallen into a predictable pattern for our introductions and presentations.

When the meeting is over, president-elect Olusegun (Segun) Abayomi Idowu escorts us back to our hotel. He looks forward with anticipation to serving as club president and is anxious to know what we think of his Rotary Club, a hint of subtle competition with the other clubs of Kano. He tells us he will be with us until we leave Saturday morning and asks us what we want to do.

Segun's first name is the same as the Nigerian president's first name, Olusegun Obasanjo. He tells us it means "God is winning."

## November 13: Wednesday

At breakfast, the Y3K volunteers review what has been seen, what has been experienced, and most importantly, what unfinished business we might still have on our agenda. We've learned our limitations in going into the villages with vaccinators. Nonetheless, the days here will be winding down quickly. Everyone wants to visit an orphanage, attend an evening WHO meeting, see more of the cold chain, immunize children at a school, do some shopping and get some photographs in the countryside.

Rotary Club of Tarauni president-elect Segun tells us again he is attached to us for the rest of our stay. He tells us what he has planned for us and we share with him our list of unfinished objectives. A quiet man, Segun becomes a most dedicated host and successful guide, relieved to know what definite activities will please us.

*November 13*

***Sharon cuddles Sadia****: As Sharon cuddles her at the Motherless Babies Home, Sadia looks away, sensing that she cannot have this white woman as a mother.*

Coincidentally, the first stop he has planned is the orphanage where the Rotaractors have elected to donate the bag of used clothing we gave them last Sunday afternoon, a place named Motherless Babies Home—opposite Nassarawa Hospital. Some of the Rotaractors are with us for the event. Sharon has instant rapport with a sweet little girl in a pink hat, Sadia, holding and cuddling her until we leave.

In deference to us, their visitors, the Rotaractors give the used clothing back to us, insisting that Barbara present it to the woman in charge of the orphanage. The woman thanks us graciously and shakes Barbara's hand, but signals me with a headshake that she'll not extend her hand to me, I suppose in observance of an Islamic more.

**Boy drops clothing**: *Boy, hidden by the buddy system from camera view, drops old clothing on the ground to put on Nic's blue jeans and knit tee shirt. Kola Owoka, standing center: Norm kneeling.*

Anticipating a photo-op, Phil has selected like-new pants and shirt that have been worn by his son Nic. The director picks out a ten year old boy whose body looks like it will fit Nic's clothing. And, there in front of all his fellow orphans and the global audience of men and women with cameras clicking and video running, the lucky boy is made to strip himself naked and put on Nic's white cotton knit shirt and blue Levi pants. His old clothes, soiled but not of bad condition, fall in the dirt in front of him.

Karien Zeigler is a clinical psychologist. She remembers later, *I felt such sadness when we left that young boy standing there in Nic's shirt and jeans, totally devoid of any affect, no response to the happenings, or to his "good fortune," just standing there. Traumatized children have more affect. What happened after we left? Does he still wear those clothes? I think of him, standing like a statue long after our attention had moved on. Had we left him clothed or naked?*

An orphanage spokesperson tells Barbara about a girl baby left there years before who recently made a "successful" marriage to a man with a "master's degree." Looking at them, could these children, so poorly provided both physically and psychologically, lead lives with fairy tale endings? Dr. Zeigler reminisced later, suggesting similarities to the conditions under which people lived out their lives in the books of Charles Dickens.

The children have already received OPV. We look for Gentian Violet (GV) markings, but none of the purple dye is on their thumbs! We see it on the backs of hands, squiggled up arms, etc. The huge eyedropper does not seem to be the best for applying the dye. We look at each other, believing someone could come up with an easier, neater method of marking children who have received vaccine!

We visit the Gidan Makama Museum of Kano, diagonally across the intersection from the palace of Emir Ado. Viewing from the museum, we get a better perspective of the palace. It occupies at least a city block, surrounded by a high wrought iron fence. Inside the fence, the grounds have a park-like appearance.

We go to the Samadi International School, owned and operated by Tom Brown's parents, Graham and Folake Brown. The school is for children of wealthy people. It has indoor and outdoor classrooms, shade trees, gardens, playgrounds, caged chickens and rabbits. The Browns sometimes have to defend their school in court against jealous neighbors, government taxation, etc.

*Fulfilling Our Promise: Rotarians Volunteer in Kano, Nigeria*

Graham Brown is a Scot. Brian McKeown, husband of our teammate Sharon, is also a Scot. Sharon asks Graham his origins in Scotland. She's incredulous when he answers, "Clydebank." Her husband Brian and Graham were born in the same town and lived their boyhoods there at the same time. What a small world; everyone is connected!

In the afternoon we see the ancient dye pits of Kano, renowned for intricate and interesting patterns produced from indigo dye for hundreds of years, beautiful tie dyed cotton fabrics.

We go to the old Kurmi Market. When a guide offers his services, we see him as just another vendor. We are with locals; we don't need a guide. We're surprised when our hosts accept the guide's offer. We soon understand why—the place is huge. It's the main market in Kano, covering several acres, a maze of small kiosks, with pathways between, barely wide enough for two bodies to pass.

Vendors offer everything – food, fabric, leather, woodcarvings, clothing, even tiger and leopard pelts. Our guide asks what we want to buy, and then leads us through the maze to appropriate vendors. Nigeria is a place for bargaining, and the vendors sometimes find us hard bargainers. Unlike other people in the market, we didn't come with a need to buy, rather just to look. We frequently walk away after expressing interest. But our Nigerian hosts give us a signal at appropriate prices, and we do finally buy some traditional hats, tie-dyed fabric, and soft goatskin leather.

We trek to the top of a hill overlooking Dala, the LGA in which we met Poline Kaigama. At the foot of the hill stands a large, high-walled establishment that we are told is a prison. The flat ancient hilltop of Goron Dutse is occupied by a large underground water tank, the municipal water reservoir. The *harmat-*

***Dala overlook***: *From Goron Dutse, a hill overlooking Dala Local Government Area, Sharon, Mal Baba Abashe Rangaza, 60, gardener from the Samadi International School, and Kris survey the ancient city.*

*tan*, combined with city smog, has reduced the visibility to less than half a mile. The scorching hazy view is still breathtaking. The panorama increases our appreciation for the details. From here, it all comes together. Sharon sums it up:

*Business takes place, for the most part, in small kiosks or open stalls that line the roads where vendors offer everything from upholstered furniture and oriental carpets to water and root vegetables. Young men line the roads between lanes of traffic, mostly near intersections where traffic must slow down, selling everything imaginable—phone cards, bottled water, CDs, clothing—working very hard to earn a few naira.*

*It is not unusual to see a family of four on one motorbike. The main thoroughfares are paved, but many streets are dirt. Traffic abounds, thousands of cars and motorbikes, engines of the latter requiring a rich mixture of gasoline and oil that burns poorly. Dust and exhaust shroud the city. There are no stop signs, no working traffic lights, no speed limits, and no car insurance. Close calls and accidents are common. We resign ourselves to the skill of our driver. Look, goats grazing on the withering grass, weeds, and garbage heaps—leaving only the waste plastic.*

*A 1991 census placed the population of Kano at about 600,000. The city has grown rapidly since then, but how rapidly? Has the population doubled once since 1991? Doubled twice? Three times? We've heard it all. Could there be an incentive to compromise the truth because of potential gains or losses in representation and power in the federal government?*

*Whatever, Kano is home for the fellow Rotarians we have met and come to love and respect as our hosts.*

We meet with the Rotary Club of Bompai-Kano at 4:30. Usually they meet at 7:30 or 8:00 p.m. But, some members are fasting and the meeting has a hurry-up atmosphere. We present our gifts, but no hand-walk. The changed meeting time will give us the freedom we had hoped for this evening.

At 8:00 p.m. we attend the WHO meeting, intending only to be observers, but almost immediately we are given the unexpected opportunity to present our views. I speak for the volunteers. Central facilitators and everyone present are courteous but perhaps apprehensive about what we might say. They are well aware of our presence in the region and of our visits to the local leaders and to the villages. Several of them have seen us and hosted us. Poline Kaigama from Dala LGA sits in the center of those across the table.

This WHO meeting, detailed earlier in the week, has been a nightly event. Joy, the nurse from Abuja, is among those present. They know we have witnessed problems. They wonder if we might be critical, viewing their work as a failure. Will I have a

*November 13*

***Kofar Mata****: The ancient city wall of Kano has fallen into disrepair, but some of the city gates remain. Kofar Mata welcomes traffic coming into the old city on Ado Bayero Road from the East.*

lot of advice? They sit in postures ready for "a lecture." Surprised at the opportunity to speak, I try to think what Ade Adefeso would say in this situation. Perhaps, "We don't try to establish blame. We don't try to punish anybody. We just try to solve problems and get the job done."

When I say we have seen their challenges, their eyes brighten. When I tell them we admire their courage and we have seen them solving problems and making progress, they sit up a little taller. When I suggest that soon we expect to witness their success in eradicating polio, one can hear a pin drop. I overcome the temptation to keep going. I have done that which I am able to do—give them hope and encouragement. The rest of the team recognizes the situation and, when offered the opportunity to speak, declines.

Scott Thigpen, leader of the CARE film crew, sitting alone on the opposite side of the room, is also invited to speak. His remarks, lacking enthusiasm, are briefer than mine. He seems defeated, as though he has been charged with an offense and he is called upon to speak on his own behalf. He explains simply that his organization "tries to get the word out" about what is going on in the war on polio. Scott is always laid back, but this presentation seems uncharacteristically laconic.

Most of the participants are seated at the table. We are in chairs along the wall. As someone is in mid-sentence, the room goes pitch black and the fan stops. But to no one is it remarkable that power has gone off. The speaker continues, no one fidgets, no one sighs. It is equally uneventful moments later when the lights and the fan come back on.

We wonder how these people who have been "in the field" all day and meeting by night can still function. To me, it looks like the fifth day of the cherry pack. They are exhausted but push forward with their business in the light, in the dark, in the heat, trying to interpret the events and the statistics that result from tallying the day-to-day data.

Our Dr. Phil Wise privately introduces himself to Dr. Jack. They step outside and discuss our seeing the cold chain at levels we have not already seen. From Gambia, Dr. Abdouli Jack is the team leader based in Abuja for the WHO Expanded Programme on Immunizations (EPI). He coordinates all of the WHO's programs of immunization in Nigeria.

Dr. Jack introduces us to Fred W. Simiyu, Technical and Logistics Officer for WHO-EPI, a Kenyan. Fred will come to our hotel at 6:30 in the morning and be our cold chain guide. We leave the WHO meeting after an hour, for we too are exhausted.

"What's up with Scott Thigpen?" is the new question. Ever since

Jean-Marc's sputtering on Sunday about "Nigeria" and Scott's run-in on Monday with the federal health minister, we have sensed a mounting frustration. We knew we would not be his film crew's only story, but we have seen less of them than we thought we might.

Obviously, on this visit to Nigeria, *The Last Child*, i.e. the last child with polio, is not going to be found. But in place of that, we don't know really what the CARE team is pursuing. It appears that their guides are local Rotarians, just as ours are. It seems that maybe the expectations of the NID on local Rotarians, along with making a living and hosting the film crew and us volunteers could be a little heavy. Maybe there are some hidden issues.

## November 14: Thursday

Today is Dr. Karien Ziegler's 60th birthday, a day we have been teasing her about all week.

**Today we will follow the cold chain.** We are in our work clothes and ready at 6:30 a.m. Fred comes as agreed. He drives a Chevy Blazer with a gigantic two-way radio antenna on the front bumper. Like his counterparts in various hospitals, Fred is friendly and helpful, trained as a biomedical engineer to keep the complex machines running. Fred is in charge of the Cold Chain in Kano. He reports to Drs. Jack and Fussum.

We wait impatiently for our van with Segun and the driver. They arrive "Africa time" and Fred leads us directly to the closest regional store, getting us there just before a large van arrives loaded with insulated chests filled with ice packs and vaccine from the Kano State cold store. The regional store to which we have

***Vaccine transfer at regional depot:*** *In the early morning light at a regional cold chain store, vehicles come from Local Government Areas to pick up their daily supply of cold packs and vaccine. Supervisors at the local level repack the bulk supplies from the large chests to individual vaccine boxes.*

come is a depot for the six nearest LGAs.

Soon vehicles begin arriving from each of the LGAs. We watch workers promptly transfer from the State van to the LGA vehicles the large ice chests stocked with a day's supply of vaccine and ice packs. There are several different styles of large ice chests, all insulated, some with exteriors of plastic, others plywood, some just Styrofoam. Each LGA seems to have its own style. The new stocks from the State Store are supplemented from the regional store's small freezer. The latter stocks are disorganized, probably odds and ends returned the previous afternoon. We snap pictures and visit with the supervisors.

Fred explains that the National Distribution Center for vaccine is in Abuja, moved there from Lagos. Fred wonders if the move might have been politically and not strategically motivated. For the north, it was thought to be a step backwards. From Lagos, vaccine could come by air. Trucks are used from Abuja—without self-contained refrigeration. Sometimes they are delayed. In the last round of NIDs, it was said large quantities of vaccine were either lost or at risk. If reports such as this are true, it could help explain the delay in wiping out polio in the north.

By contrast, vaccine by air is said to be easy out of Lagos to anywhere in the country. Because Lagos remains the business magnet of Nigeria, there are lots of flights, and they are fast enough so that the ice packs preserve the vaccine for the duration of the flight. From the National Cold Store, vaccine is delivered to a Zonal Cold Store in the City of Kano. Fred will take

**Loading the boxes**: *At about 8:00 a.m., supervisors stock the boxes of their vaccinators with Oral Polio Vaccine sandwiched between two ice-filled molds.*

us there. The Zonal Cold Store serves seven northern states, one being Kano State.

After the LGA passenger vans receive their transfers of ice chests and vaccine, they leave and we follow one of them to an LGA workstation, arriving at about 8:00 a.m. Additional supervisors are waiting, and in a show of teamwork immediately stock, out of the large ice chests, the *individual vaccine boxes* for their immunizing teams.

Children gather around to watch the activity. A hand-walk entertains them and helps pass the time. Finally, each supervisor takes the vaccine boxes for her/his 6-9 teams and re-boards the LGA van.

We follow their vehicle again to see the supervisors dropped off in the wards where they are assigned to work and where they are to meet their local guides and immunization teams. For some reason that we can only guess at, there is a long wait at the first stop. As the two vans sit waiting—one filled with immunization supervisors and perishable vaccine, the other with an unexpected and impatient international audience—locals scurry about as if surprised at the encounter and seemingly confounded by the task of providing local guides. They move as if influenced by social pressure, not wanting to appear hurried, but nonetheless at a deliberate pace. We never see the vaccinators at this site begin their work of giving *vaccine drops*, but we wonder if we have not only witnessed another obscure drama in social mobilization but have also had a hand in it.

To observe higher levels of the cold chain before our appointment to immunize children at a public school in Tarauni LGA, we finally have to leave. We return and see the Zonal Cold Store where ice packs are refreezing on wall shelves in a walk-in freezer room. We saw the Kano State Cold Store at Nasarawa Hospital

*November 14*

**Vaccine arrives by motorcycle**: *In remote villages, having the right amount of live vaccine at the right time depends on fast and reliable transport.*

on Sunday evening. Except for additional LGA cold chain depots and their substations, we have seen the cold chain in Kano from top to bottom.

The cold chain tour concluded, we return to the hotel for breakfast. There, appropriately decorated for Karien, is a large chocolate birthday cake displayed in the restaurant at the table where we usually sit. It has Hausa words that mean *Happy 60$^{th}$ Birthday Karien*. "Oh God," she exclaims, "the whole world knows!" Karien's roommate Sharon has put someone up to this. We save it; we eat some unusual foods in Kano, but not chocolate birthday cake for breakfast.

We go to the Bennie School and immunize toddlers. It is a rather well- orchestrated exercise. Rotarians and trained immunizers waited here yesterday, thinking we'd come. When we didn't, the exercise was postponed for about 8 to 10 children per classroom, a considerable concession to us Rotary Volunteers.

The CARE film crew has followed us, working from room to room as teachers line up the unimmunized children. The children are most cooperative. They probably saw other students take the OPV yesterday, but not from white people, and though they might not understand the reason for the OPV, they know the routine and trust the process.

Each of us celebrates the squeezing of 2 drops of OPV into their open mouths, and the painting of Gentian Violent (GV) on the little thumbnails of their left hands. GV marks a child so that if he is encountered at home or in the street by a vaccinator, the child will not be given drops and counted again toward achieving the targeted percentage of children.

Doctor Phil has an experience that treads the thin line between tragedy and comedy. To deliver individual drops from the vial, a piece of plastic that can only be described as half-funnel/half-dropper slips snugly onto the glass vial. If one squeezes the dropper too near the vial, nothing comes out. Only Doctor Phil can tell what happens:

*My first vaccination attempt is with Dr. Kola supporting the head of the child. I am squatting down, not a very comfortable position for me, trying to squeeze the drops out of the vial and not having much luck. I don't want the audience to get impatient, so I examine the vial to determine if it is faulty. Surmising that the best place to squeeze the funnel/dropper must be at the point midway between the top of the glass and the tip of the funnel, I start over.*

*Much to my horror a whole stream of vaccine squirts into this child's*

*November 14*

***Phil giving drops****: Phil administers live oral polio vaccine as Sharon, lower right, is poised to mark the child's thumb with GV.*

open mouth. In an instant, a hundred thoughts crowd into my mind. Have I overdosed him? Will he develop some type of reaction? Will I be the cause of vaccine-related AFP? Reading my mind, and in the concise way physicians communicate to each other Dr. Kola reassures, "You can't overdose them."

In the afternoon, Tom Brown takes Phil and Kristin on a trip to the country to photograph something of Africa outside Kano. Phil reports later:

*Unlike the trip to Katsina, we stop at will. With Tom's help, we take pictures of just about anything and anybody. From our cache of 20 naira notes (about 15 cents each), we pay the locals who agree to have their pictures taken. During our drive out and back Tom explains that he rarely is pulled over by the police. The reason? He drives the same make and model car as the government officials, a Peugeot 504. And since he usually wears a coat and tie, he looks like a government official.*

Meanwhile, Sharon, Karien and I go to a high-quality fabric market. Segun knows this market and bargains on our behalf, but we suppose not too hard. He gets good prices for us, but we understand he might want to shop here another time, on his own behalf. Sharon reinforces my decision in buying a colorful scarf and fringed eyelet material. Barbara stays at the hotel.

As we sit by the white tables and wait anxiously in the hotel courtyard for Phil and Kristin's return, the evening flight of the bats begins, precisely at 6:05 as Greg Pope of the CARE team has predicted. They are huge creatures, as big as crows. They come from the west, appearing in the sky of the setting sun. At first there are a scattered few. Then they come evenly spaced in three dimensions, low-flyers and high-flyers across the sky as far as we can see from north to south, flying in straight lines, as straight as bats can fly in their "flap-flap-flap-rest" rhythm of flight. No one in the courtyard seems to know whence they come or whither they might go. Thousands of them pass during their half-hour parade. The farmer in me sees a potential threat to someone's crops.

Tom is later than we hoped in bringing Phil and Kristin back, but when we hear their report, we are grateful for their return. Some picture-taking events had threatened to turn ugly. Kristin:

*Nigeria has intrigued me for years. I came eager to see the countryside, the farmland, and its people. I trust in Tom Brown's ability to secure our safety, and am grateful when he offers to drive Phil and me to some areas outside the City of Kano.*

*We have a long list of images that will build a pictorial story for Tom's country. My anticipation mounts as we set out on our journey, planning our stops to take in as much as possible.*

*November 14*

*The images are powerful: roadside stands carefully tended, elderly women crouched with arms outstretched, begging for anything at all, meat markets where flies swarm on cuts of meat and on severed goat heads that have been lying for days in the tropical heat. The scenes and vibrant colors that fill my viewfinder are sensational.*

*We travel to an area that Tom is certain will be rewarding. "The Fulani people are of a different character," Tom shares. "They are gentle and soft-spoken, people who tend to keep to themselves."*

*Tom is right. My encounter with a Fulani herdsman and his cattle is one of the most prominent images of the day, perhaps of the week. He is beautiful, sincere, and genuine—a memory that I shall hold dear.*

*The markets are possibly my favorite subject: contrasting colors of the carefully stacked fruits, vegetables, and beautiful robes of the men and women tending the stands. We stop at a market quite some distance from the city. The variety of wares is much larger than in other markets we have visited. Tom has prepared us that we might need to entice some of the people with payments, encouraging them to be photographed. We have a supply of small bills in Naira, the Nigerian currency.*

*I become overwhelmed with opportunities. In every direction that I turn there is yet another image I want to capture. Tom has been negotiating our photo-ops, mentioning that we are visitors from Russia. He seems uncomfortable identifying us as Americans.*

*Suddenly, Tom's tone changes. There is urgency in his voice. Someone in the crowd has yelled something threatening. Tom responds in their native language, unfamiliar to Phil and me. At first, he encourages calmly, "Get in the car, Kristin." Finally, he orders, "Kristin, GET IN THE CAR!"*

*As we get back to his car, a mob is forming around us. There seems to be confusion as to who should receive the Naira we handed out for the pho-*

*Fulfilling Our Promise: Rotarians Volunteer in Kano, Nigeria*

**Fulani herdsman**: *In a visit among Fulani farmers, Kris captures the spirit of a herdsman with his healthy cattle.*

**Tilling by hand**: *Food production, harvesting, and marketing, consumes a large proportion of the Nigerian labor resource.*

*November 14*

*tos. The men from the market are fighting amongst themselves, ripping at the bills as we try to get into Tom's car. There is shouting and shoving as Tom locks the doors and tries to pull away. Arms come flailing and grabbing through the windows as we try to roll them up.*

*Tom has been scratched by someone in the crowd and he is visibly shaken, concerned about being infected with aids. He talks about going to the hospital immediately to be tested.*

*Having no idea that our presence would make the market so volatile, it wasn't immediately evident to me how dangerous the situation had become. But Tom is clearly shaken and the farther we travel from the market, the more frightened I am.*

*I welcome the sight of the hotel and of our other team members—waiting, entertained by bats flying overhead. It feels wonderful to be safely back in their company.*

We have a birthday dinner for DRZ as Dr. Karien Ziegler is known among her professional colleagues. The CARE film crew joins us, along with Segun our Rotarian host, and Jillian Barth, a woman from the British High Command. There is the big chocolate cake with candles, singing, a birthday card and a crown fashioned from colored-tinsel pipe cleaners provided by Joy DeBendetto, the CNN journalist traveling as part of the CARE film crew. We miss only Jean-Marc Giboux, the photographer sent by RI in Evanston. He has cleared out.

The Calypso Restaurant at the Prince Hotel always serves good food and generous portions, but it is also an ordeal at every meal to get our bills and to get change after paying. No matter that we have asked the waiters to bring our bills, we experience the usual delays. The Nigerian word for tip is *dash*. We don't know the custom here. Maybe if we gave the tip up front, the waiters would dash for our bill?

*Fulfilling Our Promise: Rotarians Volunteer in Kano, Nigeria*

**The Volunteers Dress Up**: *The team honors Karien, left, by dressing up on the occasion of her birthday.*

On account of the birthday celebration, my team mutinies tonight against the yellow tee shirts, putting on fancy clothes they have either paid good money for here in Nigeria or brought all the way from North America. They will not be denied, and I envy them. Since I have nothing else, it is my lot as team leader to wear the team uniform yellow tee shirt. It has a nice blue collar. So, I put on a blue Rotary tie and suck it up. "My team" looks so good. We stop on the way to the Rotary meeting for a photo. It is a good thing, for a clothing surprise awaits them, and no other evidence will exist that they ever really dressed up.

*November 14*

The Rotary Club of Nasarawa-Kano waits, and when we arrive, club president Sunday (Sunny) Nneji moves the meeting promptly along. There are Rotarians here whom we have seen at the other Rotary meetings during the week. They've put in more time on our behalf this week than we should ever expect. We present our remaining two bags of children's clothing and the immunization prizes, acknowledging that the latter might have to be saved for the next round of NIDs.

The Rotarians honor Dr. Karien again for her birthday, and then decorate all of us in new "team uniforms," colorful, traditional, tribal—Fulani hunter's garb—over everyone's fancy clothes. President Sunny's business is Sunnytex Textiles Co. Nig. Ltd. We wonder if there is a connection. Good humor and energetic participation of many members characterizes the meeting. When all the members of Y3K sing together both the U.S. and Canadian national anthems, president Sunny remarks, tongue in cheek, "The United States and Canada must be one country with two national songs."

Tom Brown brings to our hotel the items that we picked out Monday night at the market across the street from the Central Hotel. We pay him and he settles our accounts with the vendors.

*Fulfilling Our Promise: Rotarians Volunteer in Kano, Nigeria*

**Surveillance Pickup**: *Utility vehicles, motorcycles, two way radios, computers and generators are among the pieces of heavy artillery in the war on polio. Norm sits in this disease surveillance vehicle, donated by Rotary International thru the World Health Organization.*

# GETTING THE JOB DONE

Four well-known organizations—the World Health Organization (WHO), Rotary International (RI), U.S. Centers for Disease Control (CDC), and UNICEF—are the partners in spearheading the Global Polio Eradication Initiative (GPEI). There are other key partners. Some are governments, some are non-governmental organizations (NGOs).

Rotarians generally feel that Rotary is slighted in recognition for its role. Maybe, but the gigantic polio initiative can succeed only with a lot of money and influence on board—foundations like those of Bill and Melinda Gates, the United Nations, OPEC and multinational corporations, or agencies like the World Bank and the European Union.

NGOs like the International Red Cross, Red Crescent, Save the Children, CORE, CARE, and others make significant impacts. Scott Thigpen's CARE film team is an example. Many play a unique role in accessing the children in hard to reach areas such as in conflict-affected countries. Only through the efforts of Interagency Coordinating Committees (ICCs) can the necessary consensus be reached for important decisions and for program administration.

Expanded Programs of Immunization (EPI) is an effort at the national level in individual countries to apply principles of the GPEI. Nigeria has a National Programme of Immunization (NPI). Among interrelated challenges NPI has to overcome are:

- Accessing the children
- Maintaining the necessary funding
- Maintaining political commitment
- Interagency coordination at every level
- Social mobilization—enlisting, training and deploying

- sufficient human resources
- Assuring an adequate total supply of vaccine
- Maintaining cold chains and delivery to right places, right times
- Communicating accurately and adequately with all

In our short mission, we have witnessed courageous leaders confront almost every challenge on the list—a collaborative effort to make things work at each level of administration. At the international and national levels, it is a committee of officials from different agencies.

It is no less complicated in the 36 states, 774 Local Government Areas, and over 5,400 wards across Nigeria. Health leaders must deal with elected officials, traditional leaders, appointed officials and temporary recruits who are all influenced by economic incentives, as well as religious and tribal loyalties that vary widely from place to place.

Religion is an ancient and integral part of culture in Nigeria. While European-style Christianity is superimposed over traditional beliefs in the South, Arab-style Islam is superimposed over traditional beliefs in the North. Particularly in Islamic tradition, and in the many tribal cultures, there is little separation of religious influence and political power. Religion, therefore, has a strong connection with both the tribal and political systems across the country.

Whether getting the job done is an art or a science, personalities like Adefeso, Fussum and Kaigama testify to the fact that nothing substitutes for thoughtful, visionary initiative.

**This is bigger than any of us can imagine. In humanitarian terms, what happens here is as mysterious, majestic, and powerful as the great Sahara is in generating the harmattan and the hurricanes of the Atlantic.**

*November 15*

**Barbara meets students**: *As a classroom teacher, Barb is always at home among students, quickly gaining their confidence.*

needs are not educated (much like children in the US prior to PL94-142, IDEA, etc). Patricia Ighile takes these children free of all charges into her beautiful school and tries to make a difference in their lives. We have such great admiration and respect for the efforts of Patricia and her young teachers.

Meanwhile, the rest of us are with Segun and our young Muslim driver in the Child-Spacing Van. On the way from the Tarauni School to the Samadi International School, we drive to the top of the Rock of Bompai. A group of Christians in white robes and bright red sashes have gathered for prayers. Bompai Rock is not high, but without so much as scanning the view, we leave, wondering if our quick departure is a function of Segun and our Muslim driver feeling unwelcome, or simply that our prompt arrival is being awaited at the next stop.

It is our second visit to Samadi International. I wonder aloud to Tom Brown's father, Graham, if I might have met myself in him. In 1967, I was ready to take a wife. Had I come to Nigeria as a graduate student with USAID as I had planned, might I have taken a Nigerian wife as Graham did at about the same time?

We listen at length to his discourse. It ranges far and wide, from his immediate need of high speed internet service to the difference in spatial references in the languages of the local tribes.

Finally we leave the office. We toured the school on our first visit. This time, students are gathering in the courtyard theater. It's Friday and there will be a special end-of-the-week program. We will join them. In front of the students in the small amphitheater is a sandy arena. We are seated in a stage arrangement or head table opposite the students in places of honor. Oops, we are the *program*! Did everyone else know this was going to happen? You'd think the team leader would know these things.

Barbara again takes charge, speaking eloquently to the students of all ages. Phil speaks of service to others as the basis for Rotary fellowship. Kristin interviews several students about the pets they have at home ... what animal, name, etc. I miss Sharon's presentation as I loosen up "back stage." This is definitely a hand-walking opportunity. And the sand pit looks reminiscent of my hand-walks on the beaches of the Indian and Pacific Oceans.

Asked to continue her presentation, Karien skillfully does so after thinking she has finished. "Oh," says the college prof, "No one has ever asked me to speak more." Then the "why" of it becomes evident. A gigantic birthday card has been circulating among the students and when they have all signed it, they present

*November 15*

it to her and sing "Happy Birthday." She worked for that one.

I introduce myself as the others have done and explain hand-walking in the context of Phil's presentation on Rotary service. Hand-walking can be used as a means of raising money or as a means of building interest among parents to give their children the vaccine drops. When I finally start, the sand pit is more of a challenge than I expected. I have to pick my hands straight up and put them straight down. Scuffing them forward kicks dust and sand into my face.

As the custom has evolved in the Rotary meetings, my team starts counting the steps. Half way around the pit, 25 steps. All the way around, 55 steps. Steps are getting smaller. I stumble on a high spot at 68 and after regaining control, give up at 72. The students respond affirmatively. As usual, several approach me and want me to tell them the secret of hand-walking.

I ask them how long it took them to first walk on their feet. Are you willing to work at it every day for almost a year? Okay, put your feet up against a wall and get the feel of being upside down. Make your shoulders and arms strong. Try to balance on your hands without using the wall. In less than a year, you'll be walking on your hands.

The CARE team is present. They do their closing interview with Kristin; the garden atmosphere of the school is the perfect setting. We bid the Browns farewell and return to the hotel.

The film crew is departing. We hate to see them go, but they are eager. They have not had the warm and affectionate people-to-people experience we have had. They came here frustrated that the eradication of polio is behind schedule. They sought the reasons. One might say they came looking for trouble and, whether by design or by accident, they found it. Grep Pope confirms,

*There were many disappointing moments during our Nigeria trip...We have traveled around the world on this project, working with groups likes WHO, CDC, UNICEF, World Vision, CARE, and USAID, and nowhere else have we encountered such unbelievable difficulty....*

At the pool, we become a film team. I "teach" Phil to hand-walk as Barbara shoots the video. With me supporting his legs for balance, Phil walks on his hands, Barb framing it so that I am out of the picture. Phil appears on film to be unassisted—mastering the exercise. We are a team!

We clean up again and go to the WHO Secretariat at the Tahir Guest House. We have listened to local opinions about the NIDs. We know the experience of locals is limited and we have learned to recognize certain biases and stereotypes that they commonly feed into the conversation. We hope that Dr. Fussum, who has listened to the reports of central facilitators all week, and who has the statistics from the written reports, will give us his five-minute assessment of this NID in "the North." We know he has things to do; he must be exhausted from the long grueling hours of the week. He is occupied when we arrive and another person waits ahead of us. But, quickly dispatching them, Dr. Fussum invites us in.

He tells us about himself. He has put 14 years of his life into polio eradication efforts, commanding NIDs from the Philippines to all over Africa. He says that because he has been gone so much from home two of his children do not recognize him as their father. Our presence at numerous sites has been discussed in his daily report meetings. His discourse and answers to our questions are candid and in the lingo of the NID. He brings up screens on his laptop showing maps of AFP and WPV cases. He tells us the outcome of follow-up efforts in problem areas.

Four LGAs are targeted for an intense mop-up effort. "The exercise" has been extended there for two days and he will send 23 of his best supervisors and international consultants. They'll have 11 vehicles at their disposal. Social mobilization strategies have already been implemented. All the traditional local leaders have been invited to be on board. Even so, cooperation professed by the local leaders does not always translate into active and effective participation. But you have to ask, and nothing succeeds like peer pressure. The efforts have paid off in other countries. They will here too.

The cold chain will stay in place to serve for two additional days. Immunization teams and supervisors will not be paid until the mop-up is done, the equipment turned in, and the reports completed. For the war on polio, Fussum's office is a command center in every sense. He has both infantry and heavy artillery at his disposal. Benefactors of the War on Polio can take comfort in the manner in which this General prosecutes the war.

Dr. Fussum's bottom line, which is what we had originally come to hear, seems to be that in spite of the difficulties, this NID has gone much better than the last one. It's a given that there must be more NIDs in Nigeria, but the momentum is moving toward a conclusion. The WPV cases are being pinpointed and identified by DNA mapping. The reservoirs of WPV are showing evidence of confinement and no doubt, with a continued focus, the end of polio is achievable in the near future.

Our reception by Dr. Fussum seems to speak volumes about his view of us. He characterizes most volunteers (meaning people like us) as arriving late and leaving early for NIDs. But, he seems to imply, "present company excepted." He gives us one and one quarter hours before we finally take the initiative to end the meeting.

We return to the hotel and hold a team dinner. We have become like family. Sharon asked earlier if she might share with us one of her family traditions. We gave her the go-ahead and now we will find out what our mirthful Canadian has in store. She explains that with her family all vacations end with an awards ceremony; this isn't a vacation, but this week we are her family.

Everyone is thrilled and complimented as she gives each of us a thoughtfully chosen personal prize. Kristin receives the "You've Got Heart, Girl" award in recognition of her determination to participate even after she had spent a sleepless night in the bathroom. She gives Phil the "Entertainer" award, not needing to, and best that she not, explain the jokes and stories he has told to keep us amused when our spirits floundered, or when we missed our real families.

Karien, Sharon's roommate, gets the "Best Roommate in the World" award. And, Barb, the award for "Outstanding Communicator." Her teaching skills and experience have trained her to communicate with well-chosen words, gestures, songs, and a winning smile. Sharon embarrasses me to tears with praise as "Leader of the Band." She says my decisiveness and inquisitiveness created opportunities for the team in a quiet but determined way.

Our team had an agreeable, in fact pleasing, disposition from the start. But Sharon is like string, wrapping herself around all of us, tying us tight. This Canadian is affectionate. She is wrapped in the bonds of Rotary Youth Exchange and Group Study Exchange, full of the feelings that have helped shape our identity this week. Sharon reflects:

*We are blessed by the opportunity to participate in this round of NIDs, especially as part of this team. Without knowledge of the other teams, we are convinced that no experience could surpass ours, professionally*

November 15

***Dr. Fussum with laptop***: *As exhaustion from the marathon of the NIDs creeps up on secretary Josephine, Dr. Daniel Fussum a WHO official shares data from his laptop with North American Rotary Volunteers Phil, Karien and Kris.*

*or personally. We came to Nigeria prepared to spend five to seven days immunizing children against polio. Our experience has been so much broader. We witnessed political wrangling, traced the cold chain, attended WHO review meetings, encouraged and supported PolioPlus workers and volunteers, and even had some forgettable scrapes with danger. Fellow Rotarians have showered us with hospitality, care, and attention.*

*We had the privilege of a palace audience with the Emir of Kano and visits to Muslim homes. Among the diverse and expansive experiences, we also reflect on the morning call to prayer. We all heard it—pre-sunrise mystic chants emanating from loud speakers at the mosques, reminding us where we were, why we were here, helping us center our focus for each day, even before our eyes were open.*

Amidst the serious thoughts, we are relaxed. Tom Brown joins us and is much amused by our candor and loose humor.

When we return to the courtyard, several local Rotaractors and Rotarians are standing by, some hoping to score assistance for club projects, most clinging to the bonds of fellowship forged in our week together.

Eventually, we excuse ourselves and pack for the return trip.

## November 16: Saturday

PDG Kola Owoka, Segun Idowu, and Tom Brown (with other loyal and attentive hosts) arrive early. It's another dry Kano morning, pleasantly cool in the early morning light. We are comfortable at 55-60 degrees in our team tee shirts. When they are not dressed in traditional robes, our hosts wear sweatshirts or sweaters at these temperatures. They have us loaded by 7:00 a.m. and on our way to the airport.

As we enter the airport gate, an officer tries to flag us down for money. Segun speaks in Hausa to our driver, meanwhile shaking his head "no" to the official. Pointing to the six of us in the back of the van, he says, "Rotary, Rotary." Our driver keeps going and nothing comes of it. This scene has played out several times during the week and we really have not thought much about it. But we remember how Jean-Marc's experience changed at the beginning of the week when he donned the yellow apron of a Rotary Volunteer. There is something nearly magical in it.

The last of the team to board, I stand for a moment on the top step at the door of the plane and wave toward the terminal, imagining and hoping that our Rotarian hosts of Kano are waving back from somewhere behind the glass panes facing the tarmac.

*November 16*

The flight to Lagos involves a landing in Abuja. We look for the YA1 team, but they do not board.

In Lagos, the first familiar face is that of Ade Adefeso. What a beautiful man! Today he is celebrating his 71$^{st}$ birthday, yet working on behalf of the polio campaign by, among many other things, attending to the minute details of our travel.

The humidity in Lagos is oppressive, the traffic a snarl. Group mates who have stayed to immunize in Lagos talk of doing islands, slums, schools and TV shows. Rumors swirl concerning behavioral issues by and among members of the teams.

We rejoice anew that our assignment was in the north. No one else talks about the harmattan, the frontier with Niger, Emirs, tracing the cold chain, WHO meetings, brave UNICEF spokesmen, mop-up campaigns, or the eyes of the world watching as a local leader is caught in the act of delaying the NID through politically motivated meddling. Y3K has been in the thick of an historic battle in Nigeria, perhaps and hopefully among the last NIDs in the long campaign to eradicate polio.

Idling the day away in Lagos, Y3K repeatedly dissolves and congeals, searching but not finding companionship to replace its own. At one spell, as luggage is being loaded, sensing the end, we hug in a tight circle, not a huddle, a circle. Close, standing up, Sharon, Karien, Kristin, Phil and Norm, band at the shoulders with outstretched arms, talking of things great and small in their week together. But, we are not complete; Barbara is with Dave. We call and she joins us.

PDG Ade Adefeso, 71 today, has spent an exhausting week on the NID trail. He joins our assembled group of 40 for dinner, hearing each team leader make a report. I look at him with great admiration, wondering if, a decade or so down the road in my life, will I be able to do something as meaningful as he has done this week, this year, this decade?

As we approach the airport terminal, still struggling with our luggage, Kristin realizes in a panic that she doesn't remember what she has done with the tickets for her return flights. She has put them in some safe place, she's sure. For nearly an hour amidst the hustle and bustle in front of the ticket counter, she pours through her two large bags. As the last of us are about to clear the gate, we whoop in celebration as she finds the tickets. Our Nigeria NID 2002 Mission preserves its happy ending; we're all going home together.

We pack ourselves into a KLM MD11 and head north in a moon-lit sky across the savannahs of West Africa and then the Sahara Desert. The layover in Amsterdam is brief and then a long leg across the North Atlantic. It is 8:00 a.m. and daylight in Amsterdam. With the time change, we'll reach Detroit at 10:25 a.m. In the meantime, we'll fly through the winter darkness of the Arctic Circle, watching the sun set and rise again this day. What symbolic meaning should we attribute to the mid-morning darkness and the second sunrise? Without ceremony, and with but a few awkward goodbyes, we scatter from Detroit in all directions.

How will our lives be affected by this week, we wonder. What is most important: what we take home? or, what we leave behind? In fact, what *did* we leave behind? We'll need some time to process the experience. We'd like someday to recapture these moments again. A reunion? Reports to our clubs? Our district conference? More NIDs? Karien frequently would say as if it were well-practiced advice, "*Who knows!*" A book is the last thing that occurs to us, but almost the first to materialize—a story meant to be told.

November 16

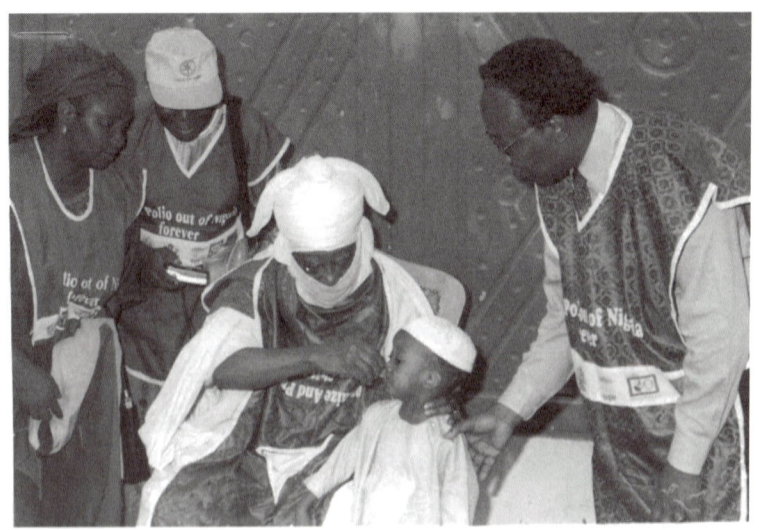

–Courtesy, *Rotary World*, February 2003

*The Emir of Kano, Alhaji Ado Bayero, administers polio vaccine to a child while an unidentified health care worker (guardian of the vaccine), National Polio Plus chairman Ade Adefeso, and RI President-elect Jonathan Majiyagbe (right) looks on.*

*Fulfilling Our Promise: Rotarians Volunteer in Kano, Nigeria*

***Veliquettes and Majiyagbes****: Author Norman Veliquette and wife Marjory with Rotary International President Jonathon and wife Ade Majiyagbe from Kano, Nigeria. Chartered in 1961, Majiyagbe's Home Club in Kano was the first Rotary Club in Nigeria.*

# Y3K Chatter: Post Operation

A month after returning home, comments from Segun via email...

*My Dear PDG,*
*The director of NPI scored this year immunization very high than the previous ones and even the Emir of Kano during his address to the people of Kano after the Ramadan stressed the issue of polio eradication as a task that must be done.*
*So we are making progress because of all the supports. The children were very happy with the donation of the clothing to them and it really improved the image of ROTARY.*
*Best regards,*
*Rotarian Olusegun Idowu.*

Email comment from Ade Adefeso to Dave and Barbara Groner:

*Your visit to Nigeria has been one of the greatest things that has ever happened in this part of the Rotary world. We once again thank you and all the members of your team.*

Funding the war on polio, Phil Wise observes...

*Franklin Delano Roosevelt had polio that affected his legs. He was wheelchair-bound, but that did not stop his ambition. He became the president of the United States. It was during his Presidency that the March of Dimes was started. The purpose of this fund-raising organization was to solicit funds from anyone for research to find a cure for polio.*

*Anyone who could donate even as little as a dime was encouraged to do so—thus the name* March of Dimes. *The campaign was effective. And when the vaccine became available, the American public was already aware of its significance. Mass vaccinations took place and polio was eradicated in the United States. So, private funds to get rid of polio are not a new thing. It goes back a long way. It is a story of historic successes, investments that have paid off.*

A month after returning home, Dr. Ziegler expressed this thought:

*The entire Nigerian experience has been unlike any travel one I've had. I think about it most days and find myself coming to very different conclusions about so many things. It is still a muddle. I, too, as usual, kept notes. At times those notes are just as confusing to me as my memories. Perhaps I over-analyze, but that is what I do. Karien*

And then, a few days later she adds...

*A poem by C.P. Cavafy titled "Ithaca" has helped me end my struggle (for the moment, perhaps) of putting into some logical sense my experience in Nigeria:*
*"Ithaca (substitute Nigeria) has given you the beautiful voyage. Without her you would never have taken the road. But she has nothing more to give you.*

*And if you find her poor, Ithaca has not defrauded you. With the great wisdom you have gained, with so much experience, you must surely have understood by then what Ithacas mean."*

*After working late on the manuscript one night, I fired off this e-mail:*

*Dear Team,*

*Thank you for the sincerity about confused feelings ref. Nigerian experience. I stopped to thank the grocer friend who provided all the balloons that you saw in my contribution to the children's prizes. In explaining the trip to him, the following came rolling unexpectedly out of my mouth...*

*"I came home thankful for what I've got, but I've been overseas before and it wasn't the poor conditions in which people lived or the lack of infrastructure that surprised me. What I cannot let go of is the magnitude of the team of which we became a part. We North Americans were not just a group unto ourselves; we were part of an international community that humanitarian Nigerians had invited in to help eradicate polio among their people. Most of the internationals were Africans: Eritreans, Kenyans, Ethiopians, Namibians, Ruwandans, all black. They were World Health Organization and UNICEF staffers, 80 of them by one account. We white North Americans were 40 in number; we represented much of the money behind the vaccine, the freezers, generators, ice chests, vaccine boxes, aprons, pick-up trucks, motorcycles, two-way radios, laptop computers, etc. We were observers, cheerleaders, media tools, part of the team, and treated with the utmost kindness and attention.*

*"And, of course, there were tens of thousands of Nigerian workers involved in the campaign too. What was going on is something as mysterious as a patient recovering against all medical odds from a supposed terminal condition. Just as a surgeon might say, "It was not my hand but the Hand of God that saved this patient," one might suppose the Hand of God is at work in the war against polio. People of differing religions, languages, vocations, ages, men and women, social status, etc., are engaged with each other in a common humanitarian goal, confronting adversities that defy description. I have never felt*

*like I was part of something so big, so good, and so far-reaching."*

*Am I going down a path here by myself? Is it just the spirit of the season? Or is this a conclusion that others might be reaching? Norm*

---

*I do believe in divine intervention. I think that's why it took us so long to absorb the experience. I spent a month telling myself it wasn't a dream. I have even had difficulty speaking about it — I don't know how to explain what happened.*

*We had the best team in the whole wide world and that allowed us to concentrate everything we had on the experience. I drew strength from all of you.*

*After the holidays, I will begin to write about it. Now that I have had a little time to sort it out, I am ready to share, and once I start, stuff just pours out.*

*Great holiday wishes. We are truly blessed. Love, Sharon*

***Fulfilling our Promise: Rotarians Volunteer in Kano, Nigeria—A Team Journal*** is published by the War on Polio Fund, Grand Traverse Regional Community Foundation, 250 E. Front St. Suite 310, Traverse City, MI 49684, download order forms for this book from www.gtrcf.org, email lsee@gtrcf.org, phone 231-935-4066, fax 231-941-0021. Proceeds from sales of this book will benefit The Rotary Foundation's Polio Eradication Fund. Contributions to defray printing costs are tax deductible.

Among many websites posting current information about the status of polio eradication, one is www.polioeradication.org.

Tax deductible contributions for the eradication of polio may also be made directly to The Rotary Foundation of Rotary International, Polio Eradication Fund, 1560 Sherman Avenue, Evanston, IL 60201.